KT-483-514

EVERY ONE A WINNER

True stories of changed lives from the world of sport

JONATHAN CARSWELL

WITH EMMA NEWRICK

10 Publishing

a division of 10 of those.com

Unless otherwise stated, Scripture quotations are taken from The Holy Bible, New International Version (Anglicised Edition). Copyright © 1979, 1984, 2011 by Biblica (formerly International Bible Society). Used by permission of Hodder & Stoughton Publishers. All rights reserved. 'NIV' is a registered trademark of Biblica. UK trademark number 1448790.

Copyright © 2015 by Jonathan Carswell with Emma Newrick

First published in Great Britain in 2012

The right of Jonathan Carswell and Emma Newrick to be identified as the Authors of this Work has been asserted by them in accordance with the Copyright, Designs and Patents Act 1988.

All rights reserved. No part of this publication may be reproduced, stored in a retrieval system or transmitted in any form or by any means, electronic, mechanical, photocopying, recording or otherwise, without the prior permission of the publisher or the Copyright Licensing Agency.

British Library Cataloguing in Publication Data
A record for this book is available from the British Library

ISBN: 978-1-910587-11-9

Designed & typeset by Pete Barnsley (Creative Hoot)
Printed in Denmark by Nørhaven

10Publishing, a division of 10ofthose.com
Unit C, Tomlinson Road, Leyland, PR25 2DY, England

Email: info@10ofthose.com
Website: www.10ofthose.com

5 7 10 8 6 4

FOR NICK HOWARD

Who showed me in theory and practice how to live
Colossians 1:10 on and off the pitch.

'And we pray this in order that you may live a life
worthy of the Lord and may please him in every way:
bearing fruit in every good work, growing in the
knowledge of God'

ACKNOWLEDGEMENTS

I had wondered about leaving the acknowledgements page out of this publication, as I fear it gives the impression I think this book is a mighty achievement. It is not. However, to fail to acknowledge the following people would give the impression I could do it on my own – I could not!

Thank you to Emma Newrick, my co-author, who has done a great job of putting on to paper what was in my head; my family, who have supported and inspired me to keep going; Mark Finnie, who has never failed to help me even when it would be easier not to; and to Andy and Mary Hambleton, who have been amazing friends.

CONTENTS

JONATHAN'S STORY

Whether it is a profile on TV, or reading about our favourite player in Rugby World magazine, there is something about hearing a true story of someone's life that we enjoy. Intrigue or concern, a similarity or sheer nosiness, we just love 'peeping through the keyhole' and exploring their story.

This book is a collection of true stories. All of them are different. Some are told in the third person, and some by the people themselves. But all of these people are on some level involved in the world of sport, from household names who have reached the top, to those who simply report on others' successes. What each of these stories has in common is that every person has at some point in their life had an encounter that has turned their world upside down.

Though both excite me, there is something much deeper than my love of stories, or even sport, that has brought me, a dyslexic sportsman-wannabe, to get out my laptop and bash away at the keys to form a book. I guess it's actually down to the fact that I have a story too.

I wasn't academic at all, and hated school with a passion. I struggled with work and found it hard to concentrate on anything that wasn't on the sports field. While no county player or semi-pro, I enjoyed playing most sports, and loved captaining my school rugby team. At a time where life seemed too much, and the troublesome teenage years were really affecting me, sport was a brilliant release and became something which gave me kudos with my mates, and an identity in school. But one crisp Saturday morning when playing a school thirty miles away, something was going to happen that, though I didn't know it at the time, was going to change the direction of my whole life. Whether it was deliberate or not, I'm unsure, but what I do know is that a size ten boot stamping down on a knee doesn't end well.

In the days that followed it transpired that my cartilage had been damaged, as well as my ligaments. Surgery followed, and several months of physio. Time spent sitting out of PE lessons, leaning on crutches as I watched everyone else get on with life, gave me plenty of time to reflect. Whether I was an over-analytical teenager I don't know, but I began asking some searching questions for which I had no answers.

What was I doing here? Where was I going? What was life all about, and how did I fit?

I had been brought up in a Christian family, with my dad a minister, so questions about God and life were not uncommon. I suppose I never doubted the teachings of Christianity – that Jesus was the Son of God who came to die on the cross for my sins, so I could be forgiven for all the wrong things I have ever done and have peace with God. The problem I had was that it was all so restrictive. Coming from the background I did meant no sports on Sunday – not because my parents were some legalistic religious nut jobs, but as Christians they wanted to honour God and keep Sunday special, different from other days. Instead, we travelled twenty minutes across town to attend church twice each week. To be honest, it bored me. There were two or three people there my age, and they seemed to enjoy it. I played along, accepting all that went on: singing the hymns and answering questions in 'junior church', but only to fit in. When Monday came round again, I used to get on the coach, and in the forty minutes it would take to get to school, I would transform from a nice, Christian teenager, to the run-of-the mill 15-year-old lad who was too cool for religion.

I don't think too many people were aware of my double life. I longed to be accepted and to be liked. The trouble was that I was desperately unhappy, empty, and longing for more.

The months that followed after my discharge from hospital were horrendous. The memory of that time haunts me even now. I had a girlfriend, and my relationship with her was strong, but my life was spiralling down and out of control faster than I realised. Thoughts of suicide consumed me, and very rarely would the idea of actually carrying it out leave my mind.

The temptation to commit suicide grew and grew, until it seemed my only option. I remember talking to my girlfriend, saying my goodbyes to her, as I wouldn't be at school in the morning. When she asked why, I explained it was my only option to escape. I hung up the phone in tears, sick with pain, riddled with loneliness. No one could help me; I was on my own and wanted out.

I'm not sure why, though it was probably because of fear, but I didn't take my life that night. Instead, I woke up the next morning with the bottle of pills still in my right hand, and went off to school.

It was later that year that Mum and Dad asked if I wanted to go on a Christian sports holiday in Holland. My dad was speaking there, as he usually did, but so was another guy whom I respected a lot. His name was Vinny – you will meet him later in this book. Although my leg was still in a brace, restricting my movement to 20 degrees, I thought it was a decent idea, especially as Mum was paying! I would be sitting on the back of a tandem when we went on cycling trips and wouldn't be able to do the activities that everyone else could, but nevertheless I still thought it was worth it. So I agreed to go, and my place was booked.

Despite not being able to join in all the sports and activities, I had a decent time. The brace around my knee, which looked more like a mechanical leg, earned me sympathy from the girls, which satisfied my need for attention.

There was a problem, though. Even though the girls were giving me plenty of time, and I was sunning myself in the south of Holland, I still felt dreadfully empty and my life seemed meaningless. I had no future, no plans, and no hope – just a longing that one day I might find out my true purpose. But I doubted I ever would.

My dad did the morning sessions at the camp, teaching about the Bible, and my friend Vinny spoke in the evening. Vinny had an incredible ability to hold my attention – probably because he was a football fanatic and an amazing sportsman. He told the best stories – the sort that would make the room fall quiet and have people on the edge of their seats.

What was striking about Vinny, though, was that he could tell me things from the Bible about God, and it would have the same effect on me. He had my full attention.

Somehow we had got to day nine of an eleven-day holiday and there was just one evening session left before the cabaret on the final night. Vinny was speaking again. I had taken my seat near the back, so that I could rest my foot on a spare chair and give my knee a break from being half bent. He started his talk with a story as usual, and from the moment he began he had me hanging on every word.

'Our greatest problem,' Vinny said, 'is not our situation, or our feelings. It's not even what we wish we could do. The Bible teaches that our greatest problem is wrong thoughts, wrong actions, and wrong speech – all the wrong that consumes our lives. The Bible calls it "sin", and the reason it's our biggest problem is that it cuts us off from God himself, because he is perfect without exception.'

My 'sin', as Vinny described it, flashed through my head. Instantly I remembered all the stuff in my past that disgusted me. Then, almost as if he knew what I was thinking, Vinny said: 'Imagine I had a DVD of your life in my hand, and was going to show it to everyone here. It would be a complete fly-on-the-wall documentary, with nothing missing. Your proudest moments; the times of great celebration; but also the times of greatest shame and sadness; the times you were embarrassed that people saw what you did or said; the times you were relieved no one saw you – all on this one DVD, and on a big screen for everyone to see ...'

I was terrified at the prospect. I had just seen that DVD in my mind's eye. It was rank. If it was horrible for me, how much worse would it be to face the embarrassment and humiliation of everyone else seeing it? I couldn't bear to think about the disgrace. It was beginning to dawn on me that if God is pure and cannot tolerate any wrongdoing, and I was sickened by my sin – what on earth would God think?

'I guess if the DVD was of my life,' Vinny said, 'I would do one of two things: try to stop it from playing, or run a mile, never to return.' I felt the same; although I might not have stopped at one mile, but would have made it two or three.

'The problem is,' Vinny continued, 'we can neither stop it, nor run from it. The Bible teaches that man lives once, and after death faces God's judgement. We cannot escape. God is a God of love – there is no doubt about that. He demonstrates this love for us by taking the punishment we deserve on himself. This is what the Bible says in Romans 5:8: "God demonstrates his own love for us in this: While we were still sinners, Christ died for us." Because God loves us and those around us so much, he cannot sweep our wrongdoing under the carpet. That isn't love or justice; rather that is just ignorance.'

I was intrigued but not convinced. I had heard this all before, of course. After all, I had grown up with this teaching. But for some reason, today, the penny was beginning to drop.

I knew I had done wrong things – I think everyone knows they have, if they are honest enough to admit it. OK, there might be people who appeared to be 'worse' than me – a paedophile or murderer, for example – but Vinny was saying the Bible taught that it wasn't down to 'better' or 'worse', but rather 'perfect' or 'imperfect'. I was sure I wasn't the former.

'Sin cuts us off from God, and that leaves us empty. We can try to fill our lives with all sorts of things, but nothing will satisfy.' I knew what Vinny was saying was true – I had experienced emptiness for myself.

'There is a way back to God, though.' Vinny's facial expression changed. Despite being quite a joker, he could be serious at times. The last ten minutes, as he told us about sin and the punishment it deserves, had been one of those times. Now however, a broad smile had spread across his face – I could see there was genuine excitement. 'Though our sin cannot be tolerated by God, it has been dealt with through Jesus. Jesus died physically on the cross, but he also died spiritually too. He was cut off from God the Father and experienced the judgement that should have been given to us. The Bible teaches that God says "Though your sins are like scarlet, they shall be white as snow; though they are red as crimson, they shall be like wool"' (Isa. 1:18).

'Suppose you're playing football or rugby,' he said, grabbing my attention once more, 'and you put in an illegal tackle. The ref needs to punish you – that is what the rule book says. A ten-minute sin bin, a yellow card, or even the dreaded red one. You have done wrong and are being rightly punished for it. But just imagine if one of the opposition came in and took that red card for you; taking your place, taking your punishment even though they were not in the wrong. Well,' said Vinny, 'that is what Jesus did for you – to take the punishment that you deserved, even though he was innocent. Why? Because he loves you and wants you to come back to him – back home, as it were. This is how the Bible puts it: "Christ suffered for our sins once for all time. He never sinned, but he died for sinners to bring you safely home to God" (1 Pet. 3:18, NLT).'

I knew deep down in my heart this was true. This was my major problem – my sin had cut me off from Almighty God. I had been ignoring him for so long. Unfortunately it took a serious knee injury for me to take any notice of him. That night I prayed that God might forgive me.

Dear God, I have really messed up. My life feels ruined in so many ways, and I have so many regrets. Please will you forgive me? I have been running from you for ages. I can't change myself. I am trusting in you, trusting you can and will. Thank you.

That night I felt a massive weight lift off my shoulders. As I went to bed a few hours later and put my head on the pillow, I knew with total certainty that I was at peace with God. Not through my own good behaviour, but completely and absolutely because of Jesus.

Life has been far from simple since, but I have total confidence that what Jesus has done for me has changed my relationship with him, and my eternal destination. God, through the Holy Spirit, has been changing me ever since I asked Jesus to be in charge of my life. The Spirit of God impacts my thoughts, my actions and my desires. While I may still not do what I should all the time, the purpose of God is clear as I strive to do what he wants rather than just what I want. I am able to love God because he first loved me; as a result, I want to do what pleases him – not because it earns me any 'brownie points', but because I love him.

Anyone who spends any time with me (especially on the sports field) knows that I am far from perfect. I do love a tough tackle, and every now and again I let my aggression get the better of me, but I know that God's undeserved kindness is all I need. The Bible says God's grace is sufficient for us, for his power is made perfect in our weakness (2 Cor. 12:9). I know I will go on making mistakes and doing things I shouldn't, because I'm human. However, God is giving me the power to change, and even when I do fail, his love, kindness and forgiveness cover all the sin that I deserve to be punished for so that I am seen as 'not guilty'.

And so that's my story – the story behind the writing of these stories. Nothing flashy; nothing that would hit the headlines, but a real-life turnaround following an encounter with Jesus. And that is what this book contains – real-life stories of people associated with sport whose lives were changed, all because they encountered Jesus. So if you love a story, a true story, then read on ... and enjoy!

Jonathan Carswell
January 2012

CHAPTER 1

LOUISE WATTON
JAVELIN

Before you begin to wonder, I'll put your mind at rest. You're right, I agree; javelin isn't the most delicate of sports for a girl. I don't want you to get the wrong impression. If you're picturing an overweight, hairy woman/man (that's what most of my friends think of when you talk about a javelin thrower), then you're not picturing me. I'm not hairy, and certainly not overweight. I'm used to the comments made, but I'd happily admit that being quite a stocky girl has helped me. I have the power required to throw a good distance. It came naturally to me. As a result, after a brief flirtation with other sports, I soon settled for this one.

My friends laugh now when they hear I used to enjoy a bit of tap-dancing and modern ballet and jazz. But those few months of dancing around the hall on my tiptoes in ballet class stood me in good stead. The light-footedness I learned would prove helpful later on.

I guess I started as a 'jack of all trades'; I even managed to wangle a place in the local football team – a guys-only team, at that! The fact that I was better than most of the boys soon persuaded the manager to include me in the squad.

I was just 10½ (the half counted for a lot back then) when I signed up for an athletics course in my local area. It was brilliant. Not only that, but it confirmed in my young mind that javelin was the sport for me. After what was a tiring but really fun and helpful week of athletics, I decided I would sign up at my local club. Athletics often isn't the most glamorous of sports available, especially at amateur level, but I wasn't there for glitz or glamour. I was there because I loved taking part. The fact that I was pretty good helped, too.

I paid my subs and filled out my contact details. I was now a fully fledged member of Wimborne AC. I even ordered a team vest, so I would look the part. This was not just a passing phase I would grow out of. Each week my dad, who happened to be a coach, and I would head down to the track, and train. I remember one particular cold and very wet night after school. The turnout was poor, but I was there, eager to learn, to develop and to achieve success in my sport. Rain or shine, I was out on the field.

Physical activity had always been a big part of my life. I simply love sport, almost more than anything. Watching it, playing it, talking about it: you name it, I was keen to do it. But by the time my affair with sport reached javelin, it was something else. I was in love! I was determined to give javelin a good go and become the best that I could.

I trained hard, giving it all I had. I was determined to be the best. Size zero wasn't on the agenda for me. While my friends might have been anxiously watching their calorie intake down to the last digit, I was quite happy the way I was. After all, it was helping me do what I loved. Power wasn't the issue for me, unlike other girls my age, so instead I could work on my technique, a welcome head start. Ensuring my centre of gravity was correct when at the transition, working on my speed, release and grip – it was all part of my routine at training sessions.

It was perhaps because of this fortunate but generous head start that I soon became the UK all-time record holder for the javelin – for both under-13 and under-15 age groups. I nearly got the under-17 record too. Not wanting to be greedy, I settled for second place. I wish I had got first, though; who wouldn't? I loved the success coming my way, and what naturally followed: the accolade of other athletes, my peers, parents and friends. It felt good. The problem was, *I* didn't …

Something got my attention, and it bugged me. People in church looked annoyingly pleased with something. They looked like the 'cat that had got the cream'. They had something I didn't. The Christians around me were annoyingly happy, *all* the time. It irritated me. Not because I was angry with *them*, but because I was jealous. I didn't know what they had, but I wanted it. They looked like the people in the game shows who wave their arms around showing off their prizes, with huge smiles – although these weren't faked or forced.

Why wasn't I happy? I was 13 or so by now, achieving things in my sport far beyond my age category, and yet I felt dissatisfied. I wanted more. People my age weren't meant to be caught up with issues like this, were they? Surely the extent of my worries should be keeping my room tidy, unreasonable amounts of homework, and saving up pocket money for a shopping trip on Saturday. (OK, and maybe the odd boy or two.)

I was part of a church group at the time, as well as the usual youth clubs that churches seem to run. My dad encouraged me to go along with my brother. Whether it was an easy baby-sitting service or just a chance to get us out of the house I don't know, but I didn't complain. The club was good fun. We played a load of games, they gave us mountains of sweets, and what was more, I got to play football with the older lads after the club was finished. I wasn't bothered that Dad made me go. I enjoyed it.

A different leader would talk each week about something to do with God. They would start with a funny story or a piece of entertainment to get our attention before going on to the 'God slot', as we called it. The fun bit at the start was good, and certainly got me listening, but when they started with the God talk I began to switch off and think about the javelin, practising, mentally, my run-up, release and follow-through.

Drifting in and out of my dream world, I would tune back in occasionally and hear them talking about Jesus, his love and how we should respond to what he had done. 'What has he done, though?' I wondered. I knew, obviously, that Jesus died an unusual death, but I didn't understand why. Was he not just a significant guy in history who did remarkable things?

And on the love issue: I knew what it was to be in love, of course – sport was my 'lover', I guess. It made sense. God didn't. Certainly not to the extent of being in love. Madness.

I tried to forget about it because it creeped me out a little bit, but the more I tried to erase it from my mind, the more it would nag at me. I knew I would soon have to address this issue of God and being in love; even at my young age I knew I wouldn't just grow out of it. The following week I decided I'd try listening past the two-minute 'funny' at the start of the talk. The leader would need to be good, though, because my attention span was short. In fact, the leaders were good several weeks in a row. I was quite surprised! I didn't like all they were saying, but it did make some sense.

I had to do something. I knew it. But I wasn't entirely sure what that 'something' was. As I sat towards the back of the room, week by week, my pride was being chipped away until it came to the point where I became convinced that I needed to ask for God's help. But what could I say to him? It wasn't like I could ask him over to dinner, or have a milkshake and a chat at McDonalds some time – how was I meant to communicate with him? I did the only thing I knew, and hoped for the best – I started talking to him in my head. Don't fret, I wasn't going mad, I wasn't hearing voices. I guess traditionalists would call it praying.

'God, you know what I am like, and the things I've done. There is a load of stuff in my life that's great – I love my sport, my family – but you know how unhappy I am, too. The folks at church have made it clear that I fall short of being perfect, and that's what you require. I need you to save me and rescue me. I can't get out of this mess myself. I feel like I'm trapped in a pit. Will you pull me out and can you change me? God – I need you.'

I was emotional but not naïve; convinced but not coerced; only 13 but most definitely in need of God. The emptiness I was experiencing wasn't from a lack of substance or activity in my life. I was as busy as anyone, and pretty good at the stuff I was doing, so success wasn't the problem either. The problem was me! I wasn't who I wanted to be; I wasn't the person I needed to be. I lost my temper, said things I shouldn't, thought things I shouldn't; most importantly, I failed to love God as I should. I certainly didn't put him first in my life, the position he requires.

I don't know what I was expecting to happen, really; I wasn't so naïve to think that I would miraculously be made perfect. I had seen from my friends at church that this wasn't what being a Christian was about. However, I did want my outlook on life to change. I knew I needed to be changed on the inside in order for my actions to be affected. And God did begin to change me, as I gradually let him do so. I began to understand that God had given me a gift through my talents in sport, and the way I communicated my passion for it, so that it would glorify his name. I wanted it to be all about him, not me. Javelin was no longer just about what *I* could get out of it. As I read the Bible, I began to understand what it means when it says: 'Whatever you do, work at it with all your heart, as working for the Lord, not for men ... It is the Lord Christ you are serving' (Col. 3:23,24). I wanted this to be my experience. Echoing the words of the famous Olympic champion, Eric Liddell, who said he believed God had made him for a reason, I certainly felt God had made me for a purpose. It was he who had made my sporting ability – I wanted to give it back to him if I could, by competing for his glory rather than mine.

This has by no means been easy. My attitude and response to competition has been an ongoing struggle, like many Christians involved in sport, and is a 'work in progress'. But each day I am learning the act of being humble and using the gift he has given me to give back to him.

My life has changed because of Jesus. My sin is forgiven, my past dealt with. My future – well, I still make mistakes, but God has removed all guilt from me, through Jesus.

Injuries are bound to happen for those involved in sport, and I've had a few. When I was 16 I developed a stress fracture to my lower back. This was my first major injury and came as a real shock. It took a year for me to get properly diagnosed, rested and rehabilitated. This was a really painful time for me, obviously, and for my family. However, I can honestly say that through the pain and tears and the wondering why God was letting this happen, I trusted that he would bring us all through. And he did. He has never let me down.

Just three months after being declared fit again, I developed a problem in my right elbow, which is my throwing arm. I was told it was a result of overuse, which is common in throwers, racket players and golfers. This took another season to completely heal. I was on the sidelines again. It was remarkably hard to take. I was not one for spectating – I wanted to participate. Anyone who has been involved in sport at any level knows how frustrating it is to be out, injured; not least because others have a chance to improve while all you can do is watch and wait.

It's funny how at times like this it becomes easy to blame God. So often we take the good things that come our way and claim the glory for ourselves, or, even worse, mark it down as coincidence. However, when it comes to the bad stuff we ask, 'Why doesn't God intervene?'

I was doing my best not to blame God, or even question him and his timing with regards to my injuries. He had never failed me before; why would he start now? I loved him, and the Bible teaches that 'He knows us far better than we know ourselves ... and keeps us present before God. That's why we can be so sure that every detail in our lives of love for God is worked into something good' (Rom. 8:27,28, *The Message*). And that includes my injuries – God would work them into something that was good.

Looking back now, although it was the toughest time I've had to face in my life yet, I would not change a thing. I believe this period was significant in my development as an athlete and a follower of Jesus. It even brought us closer as a family – Mum and Dad were pleased that it gave me time to focus on my exams, while I was pleased to use the time to build good friendships for the future. An injury of any severity causes an athlete to stop and consider their motivation. I took the opportunity to think once more about what I was doing and why. I recovered, feeling even more convinced that I was in the right place at the right time, doing the right thing. I guess my recent performances give testimony to that fact. I am fully fit again now, and have smashed my personal best by almost 3 metres. With a personal best of over 50 metres, there is still a lot more to come.

Being a Christian is not easy – in fact, it can be really, really hard. Tough times come and go, but I know I have the consistent, just, loving and forgiving God on my side. I am enjoying my athletics so much more now as a result; realising and using the gift God has given me, doing it with a smile on my face, for his glory. It's all because of the joy of knowing that God has a plan for me, and his love and forgiveness will never fade, whether I get to the top or not. I am forgiven, changed, healed, made right before God; nothing and no-one can ever take that away from me.

Over the last few years, there have been quite a few changes in my life. I'm a full-time PE teacher and work with young people on a voluntary basis at the church in Poole I've attended since I was 3 years old. I'm still throwing javelins, but I have tried my hand at weightlifting and powerlifting over the last five years, and found I have been successful at it quite quickly. I seem to be built for it, even more so than javelin, due to my short powerful levers which are more advantageous for lifting weights. I am currently British Number One in the 63 kg. class, I hold British, Commonwealth, European, and World records, and have represented my country at many international events. I am currently ranked sixth in Europe and just outside the top ten in the world.

Doing a different sport has added another dimension to my life. I have met many truly inspiring people who push the boundaries and dream big dreams. I like to think I use the experiences I have had to inspire many students, staff and parents in the community to dream big and do their best.

CHAPTER 2

EUAN MURRAY RUGBY

I remember going to church since I was very young – so young that I was often to be found crawling around under the seats! Deep down, I always believed that there was a God. However, I didn't live my life that way.

When I got to university, I found the things that were wrong in God's eyes were the things I loved to do most of all. I'd always wrestled with going to church, and Christianity, but despite knowing that there was a God, and that there was a right way to live my life – the way the Bible teaches we should live – I couldn't seem to do it.

I got to the stage where I had everything I'd ever wanted. I had my qualification as a vet, I was an international rugby player – I'd fulfilled all my dreams. I was having great fun with women, parties and drinking heavily. I always wanted to be the guy who came in on Monday morning with all the crazy stories from the weekend. It was good fun, but it never satisfied me because it all only lasted for a moment. It was like when you get a new car or a new pair of shoes, but then they get scratched or scuffed. Or like when you get a girlfriend and you think you're in love, but then the novelty wears off and you realise it wasn't real. I had basically turned my back on God and was running as fast as I could to get to all the pleasures that were out there. But all the way through I would keep having really bad injuries, and I couldn't help wondering if maybe God was involved.

The turning point came in 2005, when we were playing Munster in a Celtic League match. Just before I left the changing room to go out onto the pitch, I decided I'd had enough of my life. I'd got everything I'd ever wanted and I still wasn't satisfied. Deep down, I was miserable, because my conscience was nagging at me and I couldn't shut it up. I still wondered whether God was somehow involved in all the injuries I'd been sustaining, and I thought: if one more thing happens, then that is a sign that God does have a hand in it and I'm going to turn back to him. Literally five minutes later, I went in to tackle someone and their knee hit my temple. I was unconscious for several minutes, and had a seizure lying there on the pitch. I don't remember any of it, but it was a terrifying experience for all who witnessed it. My teammates thought I was dying.

My parents came to visit me in hospital, and when everyone had gone, the lights were switched off and the patients were settled in for the night, lying there in the darkness, I was terrified of God. I'd always believed in him but it had been brought home to me that he was all-powerful. He knew everything that was going on in my life, I couldn't hide anything from him, and he could end my life in an instant. I didn't know what to do. I wanted to change my life, to go back to the way I'd been when I was young and before I'd done so many wrong things, but I couldn't.

After I came out of hospital, I tried really hard to live a good life, but I couldn't seem to live my life the way the Bible said I should. I struggled with everything. I didn't care about rugby because my career was on the rocks anyway, and I had more important things to worry about, like the fact that I could die at any moment and then I would have to face a God who I believed was angry with me because I had deliberately gone against him. I started reading my Bible because I wanted to find out about Jesus. I read the book of Mark, and flicked through other sections, so I knew certain verses, and one stood out: Jesus said at one point that unless someone is born again, they cannot see the kingdom of God (Jn 3:3). I didn't have a clue what that meant, but I realised I wasn't born again, so I wouldn't see the kingdom of heaven. I was going to hell; Jesus said as much. I'd broken all the commandments. I'd lied and I'd stolen. I'd hated people, and the Bible says that if you hate someone, then in your heart you're a murderer. I'd lusted after women, and Jesus said that if you look at someone and want to have sex with them, and they aren't your husband or wife, then you're an adulterer in your heart. I'd idolised things: I'd idolised myself, rugby and success. I'd used the name of God as a swear word. I knew I was going to face God, and he was going to judge me.

I struggled with all this for months. I'd heard that Jesus died for my sins, that I could be forgiven if I asked him to forgive me, but Jesus said that you have to repent as well; to repent means that you have to stop doing these things, that your whole attitude to them has to be changed, that instead of loving them, you have to hate them. But I couldn't stop doing them. I was like a dog on a choke chain – the more I struggled, the tighter the chain got. The more I struggled against temptations, the more I found I couldn't resist drinking and sexual sin.

I was at the end of my tether, desperate for forgiveness. I went to several different churches, and finally I went to one where I heard a message that seemed to be talking about my life. The guy preached about trying everything, and yet nothing seemed to satisfy. Then he said there was something that could change the life of someone like this. I was waiting for the big answer, and he said: 'You have to believe Jesus Christ is the Son of God, and that he came to earth to die for your sins.' When I heard that I thought: 'But I know this already, how is it going to change my life?' Then he went on to say, 'You have to believe it with all your heart, you have to ask him in so that he is Lord of your life.' I'd never asked Jesus into my heart, I'd never made him the Lord of my life. I realised that if I did this, I would no longer be the boss.

Whatever he wanted me to do, I'd have to do it. I could potentially lose everything. I might have to give up my job; I'd certainly lose all the popularity I'd strived so hard for.

Everything would change, but at this point I didn't really care because I wanted to be happy. I wanted to know that I was going to heaven when I died. So I went home and I prayed to Jesus to make me born again, to save me from the lifestyle I was living and couldn't escape, and I asked him to forgive me.

After a couple of weeks, I realised that things were different. All the temptations I couldn't resist no longer had any effect on me; they were like water off a duck's back. I'd been trying to change my life for all this time and failed miserably, but because I asked Jesus to forgive me and be the Lord of my life, he answered my prayer. I knew my life had changed. I knew Jesus had died on the cross and taken all the record of my wrongdoing, and God had punished him instead of me. In God's eyes I was clean, and I was no longer scared of dying, because I knew I was going to heaven.

After this, I felt very strongly that I shouldn't be playing sport on Sundays, and so I missed a Six Nations match. The previous Scotland coach had been fine about my not playing on a Sunday, and when our new coach Andy Robinson joined, I'd already signed a contract with Northampton Saints, the club I was then playing for, that stipulated I wouldn't play on Sundays. I said to Andy that I couldn't have one rule for my club and another for my country, and he was very understanding.

It's quite an emotional thing, to be playing for your country. It's a tremendous honour to be representing millions of people who are all supporting you, and who'd love to be playing themselves. Before every match I make sure I'm ready and then I'll either go somewhere quiet and read a bit from the Bible, or pray. Usually I ask that the Lord would keep people safe and help me to play with everything I've got. I do pray for teammates on the field if they get injured. If they die, and they aren't Christians, then they aren't going to go and face most people's idea of God: an old man with a beard, sitting on a cloud saying, 'Boys will be boys.' They will face God as their judge. So I pray that God will spare them, so they can have a chance to meet Jesus.

Playing in something like the Rugby World Cup is, as I've said, a huge honour for me. I don't see why matches have to be played on a Sunday, and I do hope that one day that will change. But it's all or nothing, following Jesus. The Bible is the Word of God, and I can't ignore what it says about taking a day out each week to rest and honour him.

Christ is my Saviour, the Son of God, and my greatest friend. He is the only one who really wanted to help me, and the only one who could help me when I was in that dark pit that my life had become. He is ruling the universe, and one day when I die – it could be tonight, it could be when I'm 70 – I will go and meet him. That's the most important thing to me, and I wouldn't swap it for anything, not even a World Cup medal.

CHAPTER 3

DEBBIE FLOOD
ROWING

'Look, Debbie ... to be honest, you might as well give up. You're never going to make anything more than an average club rower. You're wasting your time here. How about trying something else?'

Debbie left the boathouse that night in floods of tears. Rejection was something that she was not used to dealing with. Trophies from any number of sports competitions lined her mantelpiece – she was determined to add one for rowing, too. 'Trying something else' would mean defeat, and that was not an option.

She remembers: 'I was so upset. I really wanted to do well. I had been brought up to always do my best, however good or bad that may be. If it wasn't for the support of my friends and family around me, I would have given up. They were so good to me at a time when I was really hurting.'

Debbie was an extraordinary athlete. Before she even began to row, she was a British Judo player at junior level, not to mention being an international- and county-level 1,500 metre and cross-country runner. In her arsenal of sports, shot put was also to be included. Debbie's physical ability was sublime; she was a powerful athlete who could launch a shot put at will, and yet a sportsperson with the stamina and endurance to run long distances at some of the highest levels.

However, Debbie wasn't very good at rowing. Her timing, balance, and rhythm left a lot to be desired. One thing she didn't lack, though, was the drive to succeed.

Debbie has a cheeky grin and an infectious giggle that gets her out of all sorts of sticky situations. But there is resolve and determination to match her broad smile.

She managed to persuade her local all-boys school to let her hold a key for their boathouse, committing herself to practising her technique and improving her times.

It was some time shortly after that Debbie was 'spotted'. A successful and respected coach called Alec Hodges was keeping an eye on new talent at a sculling course in London. It was there (across a crowded river!) that his eyes fell on Debbie. Debbie's determination was obvious. This was the sort of commitment that any prospective coach longs for. After the course, Alec came over and chatted to her, praising her for her athleticism, offering to take her under his wing. Naturally, she jumped at the chance.

Alec promised devotion to Debbie and didn't once let her down. Not only did he put coaching time into her, but went beyond the usual requirements. He personally drove to Yorkshire from London with a boat so that she could train every day. He demonstrated a loyalty and dedication that one day Debbie would repay with medals. At the weekends, she would travel down to London and be coached by Alec, while during the week she would train on the river near St Thomas' College, her school in Bradford. As she had very little money, Debbie couldn't afford to stay in a Travelodge or bed and breakfast; instead she opted for the cold, damp floor of the boathouse.

Each day Debbie would be found on the river before anyone else had even stirred. The lonely custom of daily, early morning practice, often in the cold and fog, was not enough to deter this gritty Yorkshire teenager. Over time she slowly improved, and felt stronger and fitter – but compared to her rowing peers, how would she fare? Debbie wanted to find out. Alec decided to enter her into some long-distance races. She came in last ... by miles. Nevertheless, she continued to train each morning, and afternoon, and evenings at every opportunity.

Despite the endless training, Debbie continued to fail to show her true promise. Then her first big break came. Alec had spoken with the GB chief junior coach, Mark Banks, a couple of times, and had tried hard to convince him to take Debbie on. He remained unsure. Having been the chief coach and selector of the British Junior Team for eight years, he was always being asked to look at the 'next best thing', so he knew that very rarely do they deliver as much as they promise. Mark was unsure, but seeing as Alec had been working with Debbie for some time, and had never made such claims about anyone else, he agreed to pop down to watch her if he had time. Now the pressure was really on. Here was a girl who had been told she would achieve nothing in the world of rowing, and a top coach was coming to watch her.

It was just a couple of weeks later while Debbie was training locally that Mark came down to watch. It wasn't one of Debbie's better rows. In fact, she was pretty bad. She was on the wrong side of the river for a lot of the time and even nearly fell in. Mark remained unconvinced.

'I'm just not sure she'll make it,' he said while Debbie changed out of her rowing gear in the boathouse. 'She'll be a risk.' Alec did his very best to convince Mark she was worth it. 'I'll think about it, but she is starting out quite late . . .' Mark said, just as Debbie came out of the boathouse.

'Debbie, let's have a chat,' said Mark.

'OK.' Debbie replied, nervously.

Mark got straight to the point. 'Thanks for the opportunity to come and see you train. Alec has been twisting my arm that you're worth the work that's needed for you to make it. You are strong but your rowing is awful – you have a lot to do. Why do you want to row?'

Debbie proceeded to explain her aims and ambitions and desire to improve and do well at rowing. Her grit and determination was clearly visible, simmering, bubbling and ready to overflow. Mark was quiet for a moment as he pondered all she had said. 'You definitely have potential, and if you're willing to work hard, we'll make you a winner. So if you agree, I'll take you on?'

She heard the word 'winner' and knew that's what she wanted. 'Thank you. I'd love to. Yes, please!' Debbie was overcome with excitement.

'Good. I'll send you a training programme, and you ring me every day to let me know how it's going. You will come to be coached by me in London or Nottingham every weekend and school holiday. I'll try to find you some money for train fares, and no matter how you do at the next Junior Selection race, you can come on the training camp to Spain with the junior team.'

Debbie stood there, bewildered at what had just happened. Was she dreaming? Should she pinch herself to ensure it was real? The GB chief coach had just agreed to be her trainer; things were looking up, and the comments of her former coach – that she would never be more than an average club rower – now seemed a dim and distant memory. It was an assessment that now appeared to be way off the mark. From being unconvinced that an unknown girl who couldn't row would be capable of getting any better, Mark had offered the opportunity of a lifetime: coaching, support and experience, with the odd bit of cash to cover costs.

The months that followed were even more gruelling than those that had just passed. The early mornings remained but the training intensified (as did the shouted instructions from the riverbank). Under the watchful eye of Mark, Debbie was getting into great shape. He was a hard taskmaster, but Mark drew out the very best of his young trainee. Her development was vast. Her improvement was beginning to show. No longer was she shaving off mere seconds from her race times, but minutes.

After finishing last out of 100 racers at the first junior trials, Debbie was one of six girls invited to Spain. 'Who is this girl?' many remarked. Not convinced she justified her place at the training camp, people weren't shy in making their feelings known. 'Mark's lost his marbles this time. What is he thinking? She can't even scull!'

The training camp was a worthwhile experience for Debbie, though, and improved not just her technique but also her race times. Last place was soon exchanged for fifth at the next round of trials, and it wasn't much longer till Debbie attained the long-awaited dream – first place. It was only a trial, but nonetheless, for someone who was told she had no hope, she was pleased.

Debbie Flood was Mark's biggest risk ever. He had staked his reputation on her selection just twelve months previously. At the time, friends, colleagues and hopeful rowers made it clear to him what they thought of his decision, but he had seen something that day when he went to watch Debbie, and he knew that she would one day be a champion.

As soon as Debbie opens her mouth to speak, she gives away her upbringing. Born and bred in Guiseley, near Leeds, Debbie is a Yorkshire lass through and through. 'Yorkshire is like no other place on earth and I love going back there, to drive down the country lanes and over the moors,' she says. Her arrival into the world was tinged with sadness, however. Her mother's pregnancy had been trouble-free. The midwife had given the all-clear and life went on as normal. Debbie was a twin – one of two girls. Despite the lack of complications, her mum went into labour at just seven months, which led to the death of Debbie's sister, Christina. Debbie wasn't without her problems, either – she spent the first few months of her life in and out of hospital. In time however, Debbie's health improved and she grew in strength.

After a short time in Harrogate, Debbie attended a small Catholic school in the nearby city of Bradford. Being brought up by parents who were both teachers, education played a huge part in her life. Her mum and dad were 'born-again Christians' and felt that both education and religion should play a central part in one's life. Each Sunday, Debbie and her younger brother, Barry, would head off to the local Baptist church in Guiseley with their parents. Debbie recalls: 'Christianity was a part of my life in the sense that I went to church on Sundays and I believed in God. I said my prayers and I prayed for anyone who needed it, but I didn't really fully understand that it should affect everything I do and who I am.'

The religious pattern of life that her parents had brought her up in continued throughout Debbie's teenage years. In some ways, the friends she had made while at the church youth group had kept her attending, even in her later teens. However, Debbie also had a deep sense that there was something more to it all.

'It was around the age of 17, I guess, that I realised there was something more. God was not just an abstract being to meet up with at weekends. He was interested in every part of me, including my rather ropey rowing. God had given me some great gifts and abilities – it was right that I should use them for him, and not just for my own pleasure. No longer was I to drift along in life, with religion being an added extra. Instead I was convinced, from what I was taught from the Bible, that I needed and wanted a real friendship with my Creator – God.'

Debbie began to investigate further. In many ways she found nothing new. From her early childhood she had learned about the person of Jesus. However, now she was learning with a new interest; a new desire. No longer was this just something to do at the weekends or to appease her parents; Debbie was realising that she could have a personal, real, and meaningful friendship with Almighty God.

'It was all made possible because God made the first move. You didn't need to ask my friends or even my family, I would have openly admitted I wasn't a perfect person – who is? That was my problem, though. As I looked into the Bible I agreed with it totally, as it described how awful human beings really are. I was only just entering adulthood, I suppose, but even then I knew my life fell far short of what it should be. If that was my own opinion, then it had to be the opinion of a God the Bible described as "perfect", "holy", "pure" and "without sin".'

A guilty conscience swept through Debbie. The responsibility lay completely with her. She had, for 17 years of her short life, rejected God. She had been doing her own thing, her own way, and she was now beginning to understand the consequences.

'The Bible talks frequently about those who love and trust God as their Saviour having a personal, permanent relationship with him that goes beyond this life into eternity, and the great gift of heaven. It does, however, also talk plainly about those who continue to reject God and the consequences this leads to. No one will be excused, the Bible says in Romans 1:20, and therefore if I was to continue shutting God out of my life I would ultimately be held responsible. I knew what this meant. I knew that actions have consequences – crimes require punishments. Looking back, there was no specific time I can remember where I can say, "That's the point I became a Christian." I can however say with absolute certainty that I am a Christian – a person who has acknowledged my sin in the eyes of God. I admitted to him that I had rejected his way for my own, and I had made a complete mess. After all, he is perfect, allergic to sin, and there was me, my life covered in the stuff. I'm just so pleased that he is big enough to forgive me. That the punishment Jesus went through on the cross enables me to go free.'

It was a gradual and deepening understanding for Debbie that brought her to the point she is at today. Her faith has played a massive, integral part in her everyday life.

She says that since she acknowledged Jesus and put him first in her life 'he has given me more than any sporting success could ever give me. I am as competitive as I have ever been, and more than most. It's just that there are things in life that are more important to me now'.

Mark knew that Debbie's potential would be realised soon, and was excited at the prospect. She was slowly edging her way past people in the rankings, and no longer coming last in every race. Before long, she was getting respectable times and putting pressure on the usual winners. Twenty-first place became eighth, and that shortly became second and first. A call to the national side soon came as Debbie proved her critics wrong. An outsider with 'no chance' was making her mark, proving that Mark and Alec had been right about her.

Over the months that followed, with the help of a large Lottery grant, Debbie began to move up the ranks. Winner's medals trickled in and before long Debbie was rightfully earning the respect of her peers, including the British rowing selectors.

There were three time trials in the late winter of 2003 that Debbie would have to do well in, in order to qualify for the team. Just a few years before, this was no more than a dream. The trials were gruelling, physically and mentally exhausting; the agony of wringing out every last piece of energy was almost too much. However, just a couple of weeks later Debbie got her call-up – a place in the coxless quad-sculling crew. A crisp, pristine letter from the team selectors landed on the doormat, and Debbie was on her way to Athens.

On the day of the final, the sun was shining and the humidity percentage was rising. Germany were the favourites to win, perhaps even doing it with some margin; however, in the final at the Olympics, anything can happen. As expected, Germany got off to a flying start. Their strokes were smooth, coordinated and rhythmic, and yet, Team GB were coming up from behind them. The finishing line was just 500 metres away, and rapidly drawing closer. Germany were edging it, but were being pushed hard by the GB team – a team that weren't even expected to be in the medals. As the finishing hooter sounded, Germany held on, just; but the Brits had exceeded all expectation, earning a silver medal.

'Wow, to be an Olympian was a dream come true. But for me, it's not about the fame and success. Apart from making me busier, it has not changed my life. Don't get me wrong, I want to be the best, and win every race I enter, but for me what's most important in my life is my relationship with Jesus Christ. In my teenage years, a local youth worker in a church challenged me about whether I was in a real relationship with God. Despite going to church and praying every so often, I knew I needed to accept Jesus into my life – which I did over a short period of time. Since then, he has given me more than any Olympic medal could ever give me.'

There is a temptation to believe that Debbie, and other successful sportspeople, have it all. Peruse Debbie's Facebook page and you'll see photos of her at the BBC Sports Personality of the Year awards, chatting casually to Sir Steve Redgrave and rugby star Jason Robinson – this girl is a star with so much going for her. The sponsorship deals and competitions around the world all seem rather appealing. However, life isn't just one big high, even for a sports star.

Those that watched the Olympics in Beijing would remember the utter disappointment of Debbie and their crew as they missed out on the elusive gold medal by 1.3 seconds. Life as a Christian doesn't mean everything is a success story; in fact, Jesus warned that life becomes harder, as people don't like to hear about the Christian message. However, as a Christian, Debbie knows that whatever wins or losses come her way, Jesus is with her, supporting her. He has never let her down and promises never to let her go.

CHAPTER 4

BARRINGTON WILLIAMS LONG JUMP

Lining up on the runway, Barrington stretched his hamstrings one final time, touching his toes effortlessly. There was just one last action to complete before his routine was done. He raised his hands above his head, clapping enthusiastically, encouraging the crowd to support him. They obliged. This was his final jump of the day – it needed to be a good one.

With the crowd still building the atmosphere, he began his run-up. Taking his first long stride, he pounded his way down the reddish-brown strip of springy track. His spikes hit the board with pace and precision. For a moment, as his arms were flung above his head, everything else seemed to stand still. Would this jump be long enough? Had he fouled, or would the sombre-faced AAA official grace him with the white flag?

Barrington crashed into the perfectly smooth pit of sand beneath him. As quickly as he landed he was up and out, gently jogging back to his bench a few metres away. Brushing sand from his legs, there was nothing more he could do now but wait for the results. Would it be good enough? Would he take gold?

The length flashed up on the big screen at the far end of the stadium. It read:

Barrington Williams
Jump three: 8.05m
1st Place

He had done it. Barrington was officially the best indoor long-jumper Britain had ever seen. Topping 8 metres by those 5 small centimetres had not only earned him first place, but also a British record for an indoor jump.

This was all a far cry from Barrington's upbringing back in Jamaica. He hadn't been very healthy as a child; a constant worry to his guardian, his grandmother. His parents, whom he would only meet when he reached the age of 8, had left to come to England when he was a baby, leaving their nine children behind. This wasn't totally uncommon in that part of the world, but that didn't make it any easier for Barrington and his siblings.

When the time came for Barrington to join his parents in England, he found it deeply traumatic. Leaving his grandma behind was inconceivable for this little boy. Kingston was his home, his life. It was all he knew, and he was comfortable in the care of his grandmother. He had become accustomed to not having his parents around, had settled down, and had good friends. A long trip to London was not what he wished for.

As he boarded the plane, Barrington turned, wiped away tears, and waved goodbye to his emotional grandma. It would be the last time he ever saw her, as she would die before he returned.

England not only brought about his first meeting with his parents, but also a whole plethora of opportunities that weren't available in Jamaica, one of which was football. Barrington just loved it. Lush green fields to play on, with the luxury of a proper football, boots and goalposts were a far cry from what he was used to back in Kingston.

It helped that he was fairly good, too. Barrington's speed was like none of his peers, and his deft touch helped him run rings around them. And so the dream began – to be a footballer.

His hopes were close to becoming a reality. He had trials with several clubs, but his dream was soon shattered. Barrington didn't quite make it; they didn't want him. He wasn't good enough, and it hit him hard. For the first time since his arrival, Barrington wanted to return home to Jamaica. Partly out of escapism, perhaps, partly because his pride was hurt; staying in England didn't seem an attractive option any more. His sister was a good friend to him around this time. She had recently returned from Nigeria, and was now trying to help her brother in his time of hurt and disappointment. They became close. The trouble for Barrington was that she was a churchgoer and she wanted him to join her on Sundays. In fact, more than just a churchgoer, she was actually a born-again Christian. She asked him to come to church with her. With nothing else to do, and out of respect for her, he agreed.

Looking around, church seemed to fulfil all the stereotypes Barrington had expected: religious, formal, chilly with a slightly damp smell. This is how he had always thought of church. But then a middle-aged man sat down next to him in the pew. Immediately Barrington took to this stranger. It turned out that this man was involved in the day-to-day running of the church. He was interested in Barrington, and after chatting for a while, the church leader asked if he would come again. Before he knew what he was saying, Barrington said yes.

On his way home, Barrington tried to understand why he had agreed so readily that he would return the following week. Was it just his upbringing that had taught him to be polite? Perhaps it was the pressure of the question, leaving him little time to think, that made him blurt out a reply? Maybe, just maybe, Barrington wanted deep down to return? Whatever the reason, he was always keen to keep his word. He would be back because he promised he would.

'For the first time,' Barrington recalls, 'I knew what it felt like to have someone care. It had only been a five-minute conversation between the church leader and myself, but it meant more to me than he would ever realise. He was just doing his job, perhaps, but the fact that he talked to *me* – it made me feel so special. In school I was shy and withdrawn, like a tortoise hiding in its shell, and yet in just a few minutes this man had brought me out of myself.'

Barrington returned to the church the following week, just as he had promised, and sat in the same place he had the week before. The church was no warmer, the pew no comfier, and the smell no sweeter. However, Barrington was glad that something else hadn't changed – the warm smile of a familiar friend. With a smile and a wave from the other side of the building, the man he had chatted to last week made Barrington feel a million dollars once again.

The service progressed in its usual manner. However, this week, when it came to the sermon, there was a different speaker. The man talked with an unusual accent, different from the ones Barrington had heard before. He listened intently, partly because he had to, but partly because the man had grabbed his attention.

The man was talking about Jesus. Barrington had heard of him, but had no real idea who he was or what was so special about him.

'... And Jesus loves *you*,' said the speaker. 'Jesus, God's Son, left heaven where he was worshipped and adored by angels, and came to this earth because he loves you. He was born as a baby, miraculously through a virgin girl called Mary. We celebrate his birth at Christmas. But Jesus, like all of us, didn't stay a helpless baby – the Bible tells us that he grew in both physical stature and knowledge, helping his earthly father in his carpenter's shop.' It was like the preacher knew that Barrington had no idea who Jesus was and needed a thirty-second overview of his life. 'But Jesus didn't leave the glory and splendour of heaven just to help his earthly father in his shop – Jesus came for something much greater than that; something more severe and serious. Jesus Christ came into the world for a reason unique to him – he came to die, and in doing so to "save his people from their sins" (Mt. 1:21). He came to rescue you and me from the judgement our wrongdoing deserves.'

Barrington grew up in a family that was too big and busy to show individual love to each other. He had not experienced the personal love that the preacher said Jesus came to offer, but was certain he wanted to. The message was striking a chord deep in his heart.

'Jesus came because the Bible teaches we have an irresolvable problem, one which cuts us off from God. We might call it wrongdoing ... The word the Bible uses is "sin". Whatever word we use to describe it, what it does is cut us off from God: the perfect Creator, pure and holy Lord of the world. He cannot tolerate it.'

The preacher explained about heaven and hell, and though Barrington had never stolen anything or murdered anyone, he realised that he had still done wrong. Although the church was full of people, he felt as though the message was meant for him alone. That night, believing that Christ had died for his sin, Barrington asked Jesus to come into his life, and he became a Christian.

Things were tough at first, but Barrington read the Bible and prayed, and slowly he began to grow stronger in his new faith. Working as a surveyor, with time on his hands in the evenings, Barrington wandered down to the Don Valley Stadium in Sheffield. He sprinted down the track, launching himself into the air and landing in the sand. He kept practising, enjoying the feeling of speed and the thrill of the take-off, and gradually a little crowd began to gather. Barrington started to wonder if he was doing something wrong. Then someone asked him which club he belonged to – none.

Among those watching were Olympic athletes John and Sheila Sherwood, who were amazed to see this man who, without any practice, they knew for a fact was jumping further than anyone in Great Britain. Barrington was encouraged to join an athletics club, and he was soon winning all kinds of club events. At 31, Barrington won the British Indoor Long Jump Championship and was once ranked number one in the Commonwealth and eleventh in the World Indoor Championships. In 1989, he was the GB long jump record holder with a jump of 8.05 metres. He went on to be British Indoor Champion for long jump three times, British Outdoor Champion for long jump twice, and he was also the world record holder for Masters and Veterans (40+) in 1996. It was a very exciting time to be in athletics, alongside the likes of Linford Christie, Daley Thompson and Sebastian Coe.

Throughout all his sporting success, Barrington's faith has played a central part. He explains his secret of his sporting success: 'God has been very good to me. He has given me strength to use my talent for him. It is important to be fit, but more important to be fit for heaven, and only Christ can do that for us.' It is his faith that still sustains him today.

CHAPTER 5

HENRY OLONGA CRICKET

Because of my Kenyan roots, I suspect my father always wanted me to be an athlete and dreamt of me running for Kenya at the Olympic Games. Up until about 16, I shared his dream. However, my life was to take a completely different path.

I was born in Zambia to a Kenyan father and a Zimbabwean mother, two years after they had my brother, Victor. I thought that this was the extent of our little family, but unknown to the rest of us, my dad had been married before. The marriage had ended, but he and his first wife had had ten children. I didn't discover the existence of my half-brothers and sisters until I was 28, but my mother learned the truth much sooner, and sadly my parents' marriage came to an end. As a result, Mum, Victor and I went back to Zimbabwe when I was 4 – though later my dad moved to Zimbabwe and Victor and I went to live with him.

I discovered I was a good athlete when I was still very young. I raced my brother to the ice cream man, more than a mile away, and beat him hands down, despite the fact that I was wearing flip-flops. I also found out I had an aptitude for throwing things, as I used to love to throw stones in the bush with Victor, seeing who could get them to fly the furthest. At school I enjoyed the high jump, the triple jump, and all the sprints. I tried it all and loved it all, apart from any race over a long distance that made you really tired. I was soon winning races at school, and I wasn't bad at tennis, either. Sport looked like it could be my thing.

My first introduction to the game that would go on to shape my life, though, came when I was 8 or 9 years old. A New Zealander called Bob Blair came to our school to do some cricket coaching. Bob was a fast bowler, and thanks to him, I discovered that I enjoyed cricket, and was good at it. However, of all the sports we played at school, it looked as though rugby was the one that would hold the brightest future for me. I made it into the First XV team aged 12, and was selected to represent Zimbabwe Schools at rugby. That was the year I also played for the Zimbabwe Schools cricket team.

In my final year at Rhodes Estate Preparatory School (REPS) I was once again picked for both teams, and for cricket I did very well to be selected for the national team at the Rothman's trials week. It was a great end to my junior school career, and at 13 I started high school at Plumtree, where Victor already studied.

At Plumtree, an athletics coach named Atherton Squires took me under his wing, and for the first time in my life I knew what it was to train properly. It was intense, but I set my heart on becoming a professional athlete. I went on to perform well on the athletics track, breaking multiple age-group records. Around this time I also fell in love with painting, and singing, both of which are passions of mine to this day.

I had always loved churches, often going to sit in quiet contemplation, just enjoying the peace and the sense of meeting with God. My primary school had been a place where the values of good behaviour and spirituality were very important. I went through the motions, but I didn't espouse any particular faith. I thought the Bible was a fascinating collection of stories, but I wasn't sure if any of them were true, or even if they were especially relevant. I felt God existed, but I struggled to reconcile that with the science I'd been learning. I had a couple of good friends who were committed Christians, and they always wanted to challenge me about my beliefs, but by now I was 15 and found it irritating. However, I wasn't satisfied spiritually, and I started to look for answers. I even tried yoga, though I gave it up pretty quickly when the visualisation exercises asked me to imagine I had become an apple.

Then one of my friends invited me to attend a Christian holiday camp. If I'm honest, I wanted something they had. These were solid guys who weren't weird, and they had a quiet peace. I went along, heard the gospel, and was converted, aged 16. I felt free and at peace with God.

Things weren't going so well with my sport, though. During 1992, aged 16, I ran the 100 metres in 10.6 seconds, threw the javelin 60 metres, and cleared 7 metres in the long jump. I really thought I might represent Zimbabwe and get to an Olympic Games. But then my coach left Plumtree and went to a private school called St John's. My sporting dreams were shattered. Without my mentor, I lost my way a little, and my passion for running started to fizzle out.

Meanwhile, I was back in the Zimbabwe Schools cricket team, and the country had been awarded Test status for the first time. However, there was no black player in the team for that first Test side. My cricket coach sat me down and explained that he believed I had the talent to one day play for Zimbabwe at Test level, and so my new sporting dream was born.

By my final year of high school, I was playing for the provincial team, Matabeleland, whenever I could get away from school. That year was dominated by cricket, playing for the province and my club, the Old Miltonians. I found myself playing against senior professional cricketers such as Grant and Andy Flower. Things started to move fast – after attending the schools selection week, where I was seen by the national schools selectors, I went to the Coca-Cola schools cricket festival in Pretoria. Just a few weeks after returning from South Africa, I was back again – I'd been chosen for the full Zimbabwe B side, the team just under the national side.

After I left school, though I wasn't professional, the money I was making from club, provincial and national-side tours made it seem as though cricket could be a viable profession for me. During the 1994-95 season, Pakistan arrived in Zimbabwe to play a Test series and I was picked for the President's XI to face them in a warm-up match. I was 18. This was the team I'd seen win the 1992 World Cup – they were icons. I bowled probably as fast as anyone else in the game, but I got called out by the umpire for throwing – an illegal bowling action and one of the most serious charges that can be made against a bowler in cricket. It was awful because I was basically being accused of unintentional cheating, so you can imagine my surprise when I later got a call from our manager to tell me I'd been picked to play in the first Test against Pakistan. I was the youngest player to represent Zimbabwe, and the first black cricketer ever to be chosen.

I'd dreamed about how I'd play my first ball in a Test match, and I'd spent hours visualising how my first delivery would be unplayable, catch an outside edge and be caught by the keeper. Well, my visualisation technique must have been off because it went wide. I was mortified. Things went from bad to worse after I got a wicket with my third ball, but was called for throwing again. I bowled ten overs in total, but after I pulled a side muscle and went off for treatment, they didn't want to risk me being called for throwing again. I went from hero to zero. Though we won that match, the triumph was overshadowed for me. If I had an illegal bowling action, would I be allowed to play again? In the end, I was sent to an Indian bowling academy where I managed to sort out my action.

However, my confidence had been shaken and I was contemplating walking away from cricket. The only thing stopping me was that I didn't want to be remembered as the player who left in disgrace after only playing one Test. Then something out of the ordinary happened. I went to church one day, though I really hadn't felt like going. In the church, after the pastor prayed for me, a lady came over. She said that she saw me playing a sport and that I was also going to be a singer and speaker. She basically said that God had a purpose for my life. She couldn't have known I played sport, or that I was a singer, so I did feel comforted. Over the years that followed I have been flabbergasted at the way things have come to pass, just as she said they would.

I played for Zimbabwe over an eight-season career. In 1999 I was awarded a Grade A national contract – a definite promotion from my previous Grade C. I was living in Harare, I was in a relationship, and I wouldn't have changed anything in my life. I was travelling the world, earning a good wage, and even appearing in TV adverts in Zimbabwe. But by the beginning of the new millennium, Zimbabwe was in an economic and political mess.

I'd been taught all my life that Robert Mugabe was a hero. However, an old friend who was a human rights lawyer had come to watch me play towards the end of 1999, and later over dinner he showed me a dossier put together by the Catholic Commission for Justice in Zimbabwe. It was all about the Matabeleland massacres and had thousands of stories of the atrocities committed by the Fifth Brigade – people being raped and murdered. This was the area I grew up in, the country I played cricket for, and Mugabe was the leader who gave instructions for his citizens to be treated this way. After this meeting I wanted to know more about what Mugabe had actually been doing with his power. There were no local newspaper articles that told us what was really happening, but I stumbled across Internet sites that showed me a different world. It was shocking and hard to believe at first, but the evidence kept mounting up. I had always thought the president was a revolutionary hero. Now I knew the truth – he was a murdering tyrant.

The year 2000 saw Zimbabwe crippled with debts, while Mugabe and his allies made money from blood diamonds. A referendum to allow the government to seize white-owned farms without compensation and give them to landless black farmers, that also sought to give Mugabe another two uncontested terms in power, was defeated thanks to a campaign by the emerging opposition party, the Movement for Democratic Change. Many in Zimbabwe were weary of his rule. Mugabe was furious, and the political turmoil began to polarise people, some supporting MDC and others ZANU-PF, Mugabe's party.

Life was becoming cheap in Zimbabwe; there was an air of lawlessness and many opportunistic criminals. By 2002, the situation in Zimbabwe had deteriorated. Australia cancelled their tour of the country, Mugabe won another election amid widespread allegations of vote fixing and corruption, and because of international pressure he suspended us from the Commonwealth.

As cricketers, when we toured other countries we were coached to tell the media that we were in their country as ambassadors and not there to get involved in politics. However, it became apparent that many ordinary Zimbabweans thought we were out of touch with reality. I started to feel that I wanted to do something to show solidarity. I was selected for the 2003 World Cup team. Now fully aware of what was really happening in my country, I felt that God was guiding me to speak out. At the same time, a Christian friend of my teammate Andy Flower was encouraging him to get the whole team to make a statement about what was happening, by boycotting the World Cup.

I read Isaiah 1:17. It said 'Learn to do good, Seek justice, Rebuke the oppressor; Defend the fatherless, Plead for the widow' (NKJV). It really struck me, because I was, and still am, patron of an orphanage run by a wonderful woman that cares for children orphaned through AIDS. I thought: 'What is Mugabe doing for the orphans?' Nothing – he and his ministers were getting richer and richer while the poor people starved.

Andy and I decided that we would make our stand by wearing black armbands in protest against the death of democracy in Zimbabwe, and released a statement explaining our actions to the international press on the morning of our opening World Cup match against Namibia.

Of course, we upset a lot of people, but we also got a lot of support – many in the crowd made their own armbands to wear. Then the death threats started. A few days before our final group match against Pakistan, my dad received a message from someone he knew who had contacts in the secret police. The message was: 'Tell your son to get out of Zimbabwe now!'

The only way to escape the country was if we could get through to the next stage of the World Cup. I'd already been dropped from the team, so I was to play no part in whether we won or lost. The night before the match I prayed that God would help me to get out of Zimbabwe. The next day, a cyclone blew up off the coast of Mozambique, and the rain forced the umpires to stop play and declare the match a draw. We were through, my prayer had been answered, and I had been given the chance to escape.

In South Africa, I continued to receive death threats, but I was offered a lifeline by a guy called David Folb, who owned an English cricket club called Lashings. The problem was, I had no way of getting to England, until an American businessman who had seen me on CNN asked me to meet him and gave me a free flight. He owned an airline, and had also been threatened by a president in Africa. He told me that when he was at rock bottom, a man had given him a loan and told him not to repay it, but to pass it along when he saw someone else in trouble. I was on my way to a new life.

I'm now married to Tara, an Australian, and we have a beautiful daughter. I coach cricket, and commentate on Zimbabwean and cricketing issues. I've developed my painting and my singing, recording my album Aurelia, and I have plans for making more music.

I'm not able to return to Zimbabwe at the moment – they don't even consider me a citizen any more as my passport ran out in 2006. Despite everything, I am still patriotic. I love my country, and I long for it to be returned to its former self. It is so important to me that one day my daughter should see the land where I grew up.

I also love talking about my faith, and about what God has done for me. Telling people my story is important.

I know that many people would kill to play for their country, and though bowling for my country was fulfilling, when you set it against speaking up for the widow and the orphan, speaking against the murderous torture of innocent people, speaking against unborn babies being ripped from their mothers' wombs and compare it to taking a red cricket ball and hurling it at a piece of wood, it puts things into perspective.

CHAPTER 6

STEVE LILLIS
POOL

At 25, Steve Lillis had it all. A professional pool player, for the last five years he'd lived the life of a rock star: all-nighters, partying and still making a lot of money on the pool table. In fact, Steve had reached rock bottom, and was contemplating suicide. It was all a long way from his Christian upbringing in 1950s America.

He remembers, 'My parents became Christians when I was about 7 years old, at a Billy Graham crusade in Madison Square Garden in New York City, back in 1957. That's one of my earliest memories. Immediately afterwards they were very excited about their new-found faith, and so we were taken along to an "evangelical church" nearby. They wanted to raise my sister and me in the faith.'

It was a typical upbringing for that era. 'Mother had dinner on the table ... Father came home from work every night, you ate as a family, your neighbours were neighbourly; it was too perfect! I guess most people went to church, and it seemed natural and normal to me to do the things Christians do – worship God and live a Christian life, and then to be the best I could be at whatever I wanted to do. If someone didn't go to church it was like there was something wrong with them – now we're living in a different time and it's the other way round; there's something wrong with people if they do go to church. But that was the way things were back then.'

So Christianity was something that Steve drifted into, rather than having a definite point where it became real for him. 'I used to go to this summer camp every year – Stockade Summer Camp. I remember they used to challenge us each year with what we were going to do with all we'd heard, with Jesus, with what he had done for us – it was something that each of us personally had to decide for ourselves. They explained that Jesus had come to rescue us, to save us.'

Steve knew he wasn't perfect, but it took some convincing that he needed to be rescued. It wasn't until much later in life that he would realise just how much he would need someone to step in and get him out of a dreadful hole. That said, Steve wasn't oblivious to his need for God, and one year at camp he made a choice to follow God and live as a Christian.

Sport was also a big thing in Steve's life. 'I fell in love with the game of baseball when I was 10. Bobby Richardson, the New York Yankees second baseman, used to sit maybe three pews up from my family at our church. He became my hero ... I would see him in church on Sunday and then

I'd go home and turn on the television in the afternoon and there he was, playing in the Yankee stadium. So I began to relate sport to Christianity at a very early age. Bobby wouldn't just come to church on his own, though; he'd bring some of the other famous New York Yankees players to our church, and he would go to meetings and share his story as a famous athlete. Of course, baseball being my favourite sport, I naturally felt like I could be a good Christian and I could be a great ball player. I had my sights set on playing for the Yankees or some other professional team ... After standing up and saying I wanted to be a Christian at the Stockade camp, I can remember having a new enthusiasm playing baseball in particular. I would pray before I got up to bat and I would say, "Lord, if it be your will that I get a hit ... "Prior to that I didn't have conversations with God!' The problem with Steve, though, was so much of what he knew about God was in his head but it didn't change his day-to-day life. It was all knowledge rather than action.

The times, too, were changing. By the time Steve was a teenager, in the early sixties, the world was a different place. 'We had the Beatles, the British Invasion, and everything seemed to be a great influence on young people. I started being carried away with the shifting culture. Music changed, and with it so did people's values. The war in Vietnam was heating up, there were civil rights marches, and the area where I lived was right in the middle of it all. I felt that up until then I'd been living the dream, sheltered in a world that wasn't real. I was a

Christian, excelling in whatever I did, and things worked out, but all of a sudden the world turned upside down. I asked myself: "How do I fit into this new world?" I felt as though I knew everything about God and what it meant to be a Christian, but I didn't know the world. I wanted to experience things, and though I meant it innocently enough, I ended up getting caught up in drink, drugs and rock 'n' roll.'

Though the life Steve would eventually lead as a pool player would almost destroy him, his career had begun innocently enough at a bowling alley, just a few years earlier, when he was just 8 or 9. 'I was on a bowling team but I really wasn't very good, so I would slip off to the back of the bowling alley where there was a pool table. Instantly, my hand/eye coordination was just there. I loved it. After about a year or so, I quit the bowling league and asked my parents for a pool table, which they bought me for Christmas the year I was 11. I was playing pool as much as I was playing baseball.'

Because he was playing alone, Steve didn't realise how good he was, and so it wasn't until he turned 15 at high school that he really discovered he had a talent for it. 'I was hanging around with a group of "friends" ... I was introduced to alcohol at 15, and by 16 I was smoking pot. There were always pool tables at people's houses because we lived in an upper middle-class community and everyone had their own. So I would go to play against my friends and they would just marvel. They would pit me against someone who thought they couldn't be beaten, and I always won. Then, when I turned 16 I was allowed to start going into the billiard clubs and I watched other people play and knew I could beat them too.'

However, Steve wasn't serious about pool, because at the time he was a professional prospect for baseball. 'The Philadelphia Phillies baseball team was scouting me and was interested in signing me to a professional baseball contract, which had always been my dream. I went off to college where I was playing semi-pro level, and getting closer to being signed to a contract – they don't usually sign you until you're over 18 – around 19 or 20 is usual. I was a slow developer in terms of size and weight, so by the time I was 19 I had the skills but I didn't have the size. So I started doing a lot of weightlifting and jogging. But I was living a double life because part of me wanted to be a professional athlete and was training for that, but the rest of the time I was going to drinking parties and pot parties and hanging out with the wrong crowd.' His family were upset when they found out about Steve's double life, and after two more pot, drink and 'date-girl'-filled years of fighting, his parents finally threw him out.

That wasn't the only thing going wrong in Steve's life. 'I almost got signed to a baseball contract right before they threw me out, but I suffered a serious injury that ended my career.' Steve collided with another player and suffered from slipped discs in his back. He couldn't walk for months and couldn't swing a bat for a year. 'It's ironic because the guy that hit me grew up with me in Sunday school class. I felt like God had used him to destroy my baseball career.' Though he had all the talent in the world, Steve was in a total mess with God – a long way from his childhood faith. Like a sheep that had got lost, and gone its own way, so Steve was a long way from 'home'. Steve wasn't bitter with his friend, but he was very bitter with God. 'I remember being in pain and almost shaking my fists at God, thinking, "I might have lost my baseball career, but I can play pool, and I'm going to play for a living even if it's going to be on a pool table."' And so he did, to the point of obsession. Steve started making money as a hustler and a gambler, all associated with the game. He learned early on that there was a lot of quick money to be made beating people at pool.

Steve also discovered that he could still carry on with his old lifestyle. 'I could go into a bar and have a great party getting drunk and high with everybody and still take everyone's money on the pool table. The bets started small, but then I was gambling with thousands of dollars. Everybody would applaud it because I was one of them. I was living like a rock star. That lasted for almost five years until I had a total breakdown, mentally, emotionally, and physically. At 25 years old I was burnt out. I contemplated suicide. I felt as though I'd lived my whole life, and there was nothing left to do.' And yet it hadn't satisfied him. At this low point, having searched for answers elsewhere, Steve slowly began to consider God again.

'Once I'd started moving back towards God, things started to happen. For example, I hadn't seen my dad for a couple of years, but I called him and he came straight over to see me. I told him I was thinking of joining the US navy as I realised I needed a radical change. I'd lived my life completely selfishly up until that point, and though I had a gift for pool, I had perverted it and misused it. My life offered nothing, and the opposite of my selfish ways was total service and self-sacrifice, like my dad, who'd been a navy hero during World War Two.'

The navy was to be a turning point for Steve. 'Boot camp whipped me into shape, and I began to have conversations with God again. Then my shipmates found out I could play pool – on leave everyone either went to the bar, the whorehouse or to play pool, and you can bet I wasn't going to fall into my old ways, so pool it had to be – and they thought they could make money from my skills. I tried to explain that I didn't do that any more, but they told the captain, who suggested that I play pool for the navy. They would send me to the world championships with a photographer and a journalist, he said, and I'd be exempt from all hard duty from this day forward. All I'd have to do was work on my pool game. How could I have turned down an offer like that from the captain of my ship? I figured I was serving the navy in a different way, but it was the worst thing that could have happened. The second tournament I played in, I upset the champion of the world, became the talk of the navy and was straight back to my old ways of thinking. I was full of pride, war veterans on my ship couldn't understand why I was exempt from duty and getting all this acclaim, and it led to a lot of unrest. In the end, I asked to leave and was honourably discharged, but I was more famous as a pool player than I'd ever been, thanks to the navy. I couldn't think what else to do with my life, but I determined I wouldn't be a hustler again, so I turned professional.'

Things seemed to have turned a corner when, aged 27, Steve met his wife-to-be, Camille, at a pool table. 'She had a similar background to mine – she'd been a Christian and then walked away from it, got in with the wrong crowd, and she was trying to turn her life around too, so we made a pact that we were going to give up drugs and alcohol and anything that could stop us from becoming the best pool players in the world. Then we embarked on an 85,000-mile, three-year non-stop journey around the US, playing pool. We played in every professional tournament and aimed to play every player in the country. There were no sponsors, we just kept winning enough to keep travelling. My goal was obviously to be the best player in the world, and at that time it was before pool really hit the UK. Now it's the fastest growing indoor sport in the world.'

In 1980, Steve was probably at the top of his game. But the problem with being one of the best was that there was no one left to beat. 'We settled in Chattanooga, Tennessee, because I developed a friendship with a very famous pool player who's also a Christian, Mike Massey. He owned a chain of pool rooms in Chattanooga and asked us to come and work for him. He wanted me to run his pool league.'

Mike Massey was becoming a world-famous trick shot artist, doing trick shots on Christian television and sharing his story of following Jesus. 'Mike became a role model to me in pool the way Bobby Richardson was to me in baseball, and we developed such a friendship after I moved to Chattanooga that we became travelling partners and I learned all the secrets from the greatest trick shot artist that's ever lived. Nobody could do what he was doing because nobody knew the secrets, and he actually took me under his wing.'

Steve's journey of faith has been a long, slow slog! From the early days of his prim and proper upbringing in a Christian home, things changed dramatically on the rollercoaster of his life. From the lows of drugs and drink to the highs of being the best at his sport of choice – Steve has done it all. But in amongst all the sporting achievements, the booze and the nights out, Steve's desire to find God and know him personally never went away. It was after five years with his friend Mike Massey in Tennessee that Steve knew he couldn't live for himself any more. The commitment he made all those years ago at the kids' camp really meant something. He really did need God, not as a crutch, or some religious accessory, but he needed Jesus because he needed a saviour. He needed someone to cure the mess, the longing and the emptiness that Steve knew all too well. Jesus brought direction and purpose to a life that had previously been successful but void of any satisfaction. Steve found something in Jesus that he had not found anywhere else.

Today, Steve and his wife travel the USA playing the most incredible trick shots people can see on a pool table, and while doing so, tell their amazing story. It is a story of great rescue, one of great joy and hope; not because Steve is good at a sport (though he is), but despite all his ability, God did something amazing in his life – made himself known to Steve and changed his life forever. Now God has used Steve's life in a way that Steve himself never thought possible.

CHAPTER 7

CHIARA CLARKE HOCKEY

As the three of us drove along the winding country roads towards Ormskirk in Lancashire, it seemed as though we should be leaving a trail of dust in our wake. We – my brother, his mate Josh who was driving, and me, just 13 years old – had recently returned from a sports camp. We agreed it might be fun to go on a little road trip together to see some of our friends from our time away. Driving there was such a laugh. We were keen to get there as quickly as possible and the car just flew along the road. The banter on the way was great. The three of us were laughing and joking around; playing the sort of games that might be boring and repetitive, but seem to be mandatory on this kind of trip. Several packets of Haribo Star Mix later, it wasn't long before that sickly full car feeling was making its presence felt.

Shortly after arriving at our friends', though, we were heading back out in the car again. The beach wasn't far away and a kick-around with a rugby ball, or chucking a Frisbee seemed like an appealing idea. The five of us crammed into the car and off we went, our hips digging into each other as Josh took the curves like a rally driver.

The songs from the summer camp were being bellowed out, the windows were, of course, wound down, and the girls on either side of me were giggling. We had set off without a care in the world and hadn't even considered putting our seatbelts on. Perhaps it was the continual bouncing around in the back that made us eventually, instinctively, and simultaneously, reach for our belts.

We had been hurtling down the road at a ridiculous speed, but it felt good and what's more, we felt invincible. All of us felt carefree, enjoying our summer break – and why not? We were young and comfortable, with our lives ahead of us. We were on top of the world. We were our world.

We were approaching a bridge after a long straight section where Josh had picked up quite a bit of speed. Mid chorus, and still slightly out of tune, Josh lost control of the vehicle. The car left the road and our songs turned to screams. I remember it all as if it was yesterday. I reached for the seats in front of me, hoping my arms might help take some of the impact and divert it away from the vulnerable areas of my body, notably my head.

On the left hand side of the road was not a nice grassy verge where we could have slowly come to a stop, but a 40-foot drop. The car plummeted. I've heard the description of 'time standing still' but never understood it fully until this point. A million thoughts came to my mind, but I couldn't focus on any of them. I was jolted out of limbo with a large bang, which was followed by shards of glass flying around like confetti. The car was crumpling like flimsy aluminium foil. It finally came to rest the right way up, but looking nothing like a car should. I felt blood on my face and in my mouth. My seatbelt had tightened, holding me in place, and I couldn't loosen it. I couldn't breathe. I let out a moan, which I tried to turn into a scream, but couldn't – my lungs were empty, my vocal cords powerless. My heart pounded and my head spun. Everything went black ...

I grew up in an average family. We were a pretty tight unit in many ways. We spent quite a bit of time together, especially on a Sunday, when we all went to our local parish church. I guess that was one thing that was different about our family – Mum was a Christian.

My brother, Seb, and I played football for a local team on a Saturday morning, but until I was a teenager that was all I got up to on the sports front. Our family was in a cushy position, too. We weren't rich or anything, but we had enough money to go on nice holidays abroad each summer, and life in general was pretty good.

Things changed dramatically not long after I turned 13. Mum announced that she was expecting again. It was a big shock but I was delighted. I'd always wanted another sibling. Not only that, but more news was to follow. Mum wasn't expecting one baby, but twins.

Nine months later, gorgeous twin girls were born. They were the most adorable little things ever, and we spoilt them rotten, as you can imagine. But things changed forever when they arrived, not necessarily in a bad way. Yes, there were sights and sounds, even smells, around the house that perhaps weren't usual, but life got a little more hectic too.

Around that time I joined Wallingford Ladies Hockey Club. I seemed to have a natural ability for hockey and I guess I was fairly good. The coaches must have thought so anyway, because they picked me for the first team. I was thrilled. Competitive by nature, it was a real result to get picked so quickly. Along with selection came the social life, too, though. Although I was fairly young, like most girls my age, I looked a bit older. Even if I didn't look 18, hanging out with older friends got me into most places. I wasn't 'wild' as such, but I wasn't shy about trying new stuff either. I did the usual smoking and drinking that anyone my age tried. It was mostly to fit in, but when everyone else is doing it too, it's quite good fun.

My eyes flickered open with the light of the ward shining down on me. I was strangely aware of my surroundings. Subconsciously I must have woken up at some point and noted where I was. My back felt numb with pain, and my neck stiff. All I could move was my eyes, so I looked round in an attempt to learn more about my location. A nurse to my left at the ward station put down the forms she was filling out, placed the clipboard on her desk and made her way to my bedside. She was gentle and spoke softly, taking my hand in hers.

During the next few days the extent of my injuries were made clear to me. I had broken my back and was to be in traction for at least the next month. Considering everything I had gone through as the car hurtled over the cliff edge, I had been extremely lucky. I also discovered that amazingly, I was the only one who had been injured. The rest had emerged unscathed.

I had no shortage of visitors to break the day up. Friends and family naturally came to see me when they could. Some came during their lunch break or after school on their way home. Even some of the leaders from the camp I'd been on in the summer came to visit me. The fact they were going out of their way to see me really touched me. Although their visits couldn't last too long because I soon became tired, it broke the day up. When the visitors had gone, I could recall all we had talked about, and work my way through the news of events of 'outside'. Time didn't go too slowly, until night came. Sleeping was hard and a hospital bed is a lousy place to be when you can't sleep.

My poor family had to make the 350-mile round trip every few days to see me. I'll never forget their kindness in doing this for me, to keep me company as I lay there. They even brought me grapes on a couple of occasions, as well as sneaking in some chocolate when they could.

After a few days of full consciousness in my hospital ward, the consultant and his posse of student doctors came to see me and my family. After looking through my notes once more, he sat down to the left hand side of my bed. When a doctor sits down with you, you know bad news is imminent. I was right.

While hopeful that I would return to some semblance of normal life, the doctor felt sure it would be many years rather than months before I would be jogging again, let alone playing such a physically demanding sport as hockey.

My life had come to an end – or it might as well have. This was the end of my sport, my life, and my dreams. This was my dream, my hope, and my destiny – to play sport.

On reflection, the morning the doctor brought me the bad news, something happened to me. Something inside me disappeared. I tried to stay upbeat and hopeful, but something slipped away from me: God. Like watching a boat leave the harbour and sail into the distance, until eventually it's gone from sight over the horizon, God had gone from my life.

Of course, when a boat leaves our sight, it doesn't mean it has vanished. It has just gone from our sight. Only time would show me that it wasn't God that distanced himself from me, but me from him. There was no greater proof of this than the speed of my recovery. Believe it or not, within six weeks of the doctor saying it would take years for a recovery, I was back playing sport. Put it down to medical naivety, a fluke, or a miracle, I was better. I, incidentally, put it down to nothing but God healing my body miraculously. Flukes like this just do not happen.

With this greater freedom, in fact total freedom, I carried on life as normal. My party life increased somewhat and I started going out more, drinking a good deal and generally just really enjoying life. Who could blame me? I'd nearly died. I didn't, so now was the time to celebrate life.

My life was about to take a big hit, though, bigger than anything that had happened before, even the car crash.

There was a 21st party near the end of the summer that I was invited to. Aged 13 going on 14, I probably should have known better than to go. The guys that invited me should have known better too, I guess. I ended up going, though; there was a lot of alcohol there. No surprise, but I was the youngest by some margin; probably by about six years, when I come to think of it. I was very mature for my age, though, and seemed to carry off being a lot older than I was. Most guys thought I was 19 or even 20. Only my closest friends knew how old I really was.

The drink was flowing and I was enjoying my third or fourth beer. The music was great and I got chatting to this cute guy. He was about 24 or so, but I didn't care. As the alcohol kicked in, I felt invincible and loved the attention. I was giving my fair share back, I suppose, but for me, it was attention without any real intention – just a bit of harmless flirting.

I was sitting on the arm of a chair while he stood chatting to me, leaning in towards my ear to allow me to hear him above the music. The room was stuffy and he suggested we go outside for some fresh air. We wandered outside and across the garden, to a field that backed onto it. The flirting continued until the ice was broken with a full-on kiss. It felt good. We continued walking, laughing, and joking, and generally messing about. Although I was pretty drunk I knew what I was doing – a bit of harmless fun never hurt anyone, I thought.

It was then that I began to realise that this might not be harmless after all. The music was now just a distant noise and we were quite some way from the party. I was alone, far from my friends – who were too drunk to realise I wasn't around anyway – too far to be heard even if I screamed. The kissing and flirting had been fun but something inside me told me I had to go back to the 'safety' of the party, and not be outside in a field with a complete stranger.

This was no longer a harmless kiss and grope at a party. His hands were all over me. I wanted out of the situation. I brushed him off, hoping he would take the hint and we could head back to the house. He asked what was wrong, but didn't wait for the answer and carried on groping me. I pushed him away forcefully this time, and told him I was going back to the house. I started to walk away. But he grabbed me and swivelled me round.

I screamed, hoping he would leave me alone, but he became violent, forcing me to the ground. He raped me, changing my life forever.

That wretched night ruined most of my teenage years. It cut deep and left an ugly scar. I detested who I was. A cursory glance in the mirror, even just thinking about who I was or what I did, brought back memories of those horrific events and I began to live two lives that I hoped would give me longed-for protection – sport and a wild nightlife. Though I was still under age, I didn't look it, and I would be at the pub four or five times a week, if not more. Hockey took up the first part of the evening; drink, and then drugs, consumed the later hours.

My relationship with my family drifted like an unsecured boat on the open sea. They watched with horror, wishing they could know what was going on. This was not the Chiara they knew. My spark had been extinguished and I bounced from one fix (sport) to another (drink), to another (drugs).

It is hard to explain, but I felt trapped by the events of that night. It disgusted me; it repulsed me. The rape and my rapist had me in a cage and wouldn't let me out, but I was too scared to scream. Not even a whisper could leave my mouth to tell someone what had happened. With the chains of rape came a spiralling of behaviour, and with that, a further cascading of emotions and enjoyment of life. I was now hanging out with druggie dropouts whose influence on me was far from helpful. Out of prison, living in shelters, pub every night, heroin addicts ... I knew they were no good for me, and not what I wanted, but their company gave me a strange release into a temporary world of good times, without fear or problems.

For three years this dreadful life continued, leaving more scars than I ever imagined it might. The ecstasy and alcohol were pushing my body to the brink and I was staring at a virtual 'cliff edge' – much further and I would be over the edge and attending my own funeral. Both my body and, if I was honest with myself, my emotions had

had enough. I wanted to halt the slide and change who I was and what I was doing.

Then one day my mum and I enjoyed a short but rare conversation. Normally I would shoot out to the pub or up to my room so quickly that conversation wasn't possible.

'There's a sports group coming to church next week,' she said, probably thinking I would either ignore her or brush aside the comment as inconsequential. I hadn't been to church since I was 13 – I doubt my mum imagined I would start going back now, but I suppose from her point of view it was worth a try.

'Really?' I replied, with a hint of surprise in my tone. I don't know what shocked me the most, the fact that the church had something 'cool' happening, or that I was showing interest in it. It was probably the latter.

Anyhow, later that week I was to be found in church again. I went along, enticed by the lure of sport. Christians in Sport, an organisation that seem to combine the love of sport with God stuff, were in town talking about the charity and their work. It seemed possible, because they were sporty, that they could be all right and decent to listen to, even if what they said contained a 'God slot'. They talked about a week-long sports camp they ran every year in the summer holidays. It sounded quite good, actually.

It was that night that I was introduced to Lancs and Rach, two of the workers for Christians in Sport. I got chatting to Rach. She was a hockey player amongst other things, but generally just sporty. Basically she was me, but a bit older. But there was a difference. She had something I was a million miles away from; she was happy. She had a smile on her face; a (virtual) bounce in her step. Whether she had just got a boyfriend, or had a big windfall or something, she was mega-happy, almost annoyingly so. We chatted for a while and exchanged email addresses. There was some stuff she wanted to send me about events they ran through the year, and about this camp she had been talking about earlier. I gave her my hotmail address – that way I could always filter her into spam if she became too persistent. To be honest though, that didn't concern me. I was so impressed with her and Lancs that I didn't think it would be a problem. They were so calm, so sorted with life. I actually was keen to hear from them. I wanted to know what made them tick.

Almost before I got home there was an email waiting for me from Rach. Man, she was keen! When we were chatting at the back of church she had mentioned a summer camp that CiS ran each year. They host a few, but there was one for my age group, and during the week they had hockey sessions with coaches and the rest. She had my interest.

I opened up the email and its attachment – an application form for the camp. If I had stopped to think about it for a little longer I would have told myself to smarten up and sort myself out. Was I really thinking of going on a God camp with a load of geeks (that's how I saw Christians)? Surely not. But before I knew it I was pressing 'print' and looking for a pen. Maybe it was the infectious enthusiasm of Rach or the lure of 'free' (Mum would be paying) coaching sessions: either way, I was signing up. I plucked the two sheets of paper from the printer, ink still damp, and began to fill in the form.

I went to bed that night and just kept thinking about the two guys that had come to talk in the church. They had talked about God and about their Christian work and they were probably the happiest people I had seen in a very long time. They seemed so fulfilled and had a strange calmness about them.

Within minutes of arriving at camp I felt like I'd been there a lifetime and was hanging out with friends. Rach and Lancs were there too and helped carry my bags to reception, where I registered and got my gear sorted. I had my 'pocket money' for the tuck shop in one hand, a rucksack over my shoulder, and in the other hand the registration team placed a Bible. They explained I would need it throughout the week. I was placed in a dorm with some girls my age – one of whom would be joining the hockey sessions too. From the moment I arrived at camp, life began to change.

Life at camp was a buzz, one high after another. The banter was immense, the laughs and giggles so intense my stomach actually hurt at times. The coaching was at a high level and I felt I was improving even in the short space of time I was there. Gosh, even the food was pretty good! Every second of each day was filled with something fun, whether it be singing at meal times, having a laugh at our dorm leader's expense, or even the 'God' meetings we had each night.

I have got to be honest, I was pretty sceptical about these Bible sessions at first. Were they just a church service in disguise? I grabbed my Bible and headed to the meeting room with the rest of the girls from my dorm. I didn't expect much, but I thought I could catch up on some sleep. To my surprise, from the moment the meeting started I was on the edge of my seat. Silly games with the incentive of winning prizes, and reviews of the day on DVD (they caught me on camera pulling a silly face – I was mortified!), someone explaining how they became a Christian, and then a short talk from one of the leaders – it all made for an enthralling hour. I was hanging on every word, unintentionally at first, but as the days went on it was more deliberate.

The sessions were so relevant to my life. In fact, after a couple of days I wondered if they had prepared them just for me, knowing my life story. Drugs, drink, sex, partying ... they talked about it all. As I looked around the room, and later on as our dorm group met separately to discuss that evening's session, I thought to myself, 'They are all so innocent. I think I'm the only bad one round here!' The questions my peers were asking just didn't resonate with where I was and what I had done. My past seemed so much darker. For the first time since camp began, I felt uncomfortable, embarrassed and like I didn't fit in. I didn't deserve to be at camp. If only they knew what I was really like, they would send me home immediately ... or so I thought.

One of the girls in my team, who I'd got to know quite well, Lucy, noticed that I wasn't my usual self and participating as much as I had been. When everyone went to bed, I was sitting in the corridor collecting my thoughts and enjoying a little time to myself. After a little while, Lucy came and joined me. We started talking about the day's events and all we had heard in the meetings. I was pretty honest with her and explained that I was struggling. We talked for absolutely hours. The gentle snoring of the girls in the dorm could be heard in the corridor.

'We'd better head to bed, too,' Lucy said eventually. Reluctantly, I agreed. Before I could stand up and head back to my room though, she held my hand and asked if she could pray for me. No one had ever asked or offered that, especially not one of my friends. It was the weirdest thing ever. Scary, nerve-racking, yet absolutely amazing, all at the same time. Squeezing my hand, she began to pray. She asked God to help me, she thanked him that I'd been so honest and she asked him to change my life.

I got into bed, trying not to wake the other girls. I sobbed gently to myself as I tried to get to sleep. The pillow slowly became damp and uncomfortable. Why I was crying I had no idea, because for the first time since I could remember, I felt happy inside.

I then did something I had never done before. I prayed. I prayed to God and pleaded for him to take control of my life and change me. In the talk earlier that evening, we had been told that Jesus changed lives; if we asked him to forgive us for the wrong things in our lives, and submitted to his rule, he would change us. Not in any physical or mental way, but in a manner that was much more deep and permanent – a spiritual change, one that no longer left us outside of God's family but brought us to know him and live for him now, and be with him for eternity.

I wanted the happiness I had seen in the Christians around me all week. I wanted to start living my life for Jesus and not for myself. I had tried living for me, the selfish way – it didn't work.

I can tell you for sure that the simple but desperate prayer I prayed that night at camp was heard by God. It was like the biggest load ever was lifted off me, and I had never felt so free. I wanted to run outside and scream to the world what God had done for me and that I was now living my life for him. I wanted others to know the amazing good news of Jesus – that he died on the cross to take the punishment for everything we have ever said or done to offend God or others so we can be forgiven. He can set us free! The feeling of happiness and freedom was so overpowering and overwhelming; at first I wasn't quite sure what to do with it. Eventually at past 3 a.m. I drifted off to sleep, emotionally and physically exhausted. Would I wake up and find it was all a dream, or worse, just an emotional decision I didn't really mean? Time would tell.

I thank God that it wasn't a dream. Looking back at my life now I can see how God worked throughout the years that I struggled in so many different ways. At the time it felt horrendous, but God never let those times overcome me. He clearly had 'an eye out for me'. He was watching, shaping, changing and making me so that one day, as I heard the amazing news of Jesus' forgiveness available for us I would come to trust him.

Years earlier, after the crash, the emergency services were gobsmacked that we weren't all dead. They couldn't believe how we had all survived the crash and that I was the only one hurt. The doctors told me I had been an inch from being paralyzed my whole life. And yet within a month and a half (before the first league game) I was back playing hockey at peak physical fitness. God gave me so much love and I had so many visitors, friends and family every single day, helping me through the time in hospital and making the weeks so much more bearable. Even in the worst of situations, he had not let me go; God had not abandoned me. Though I had walked away from him and was living my own life, he was still interested in me, still wanting me to come 'home'.

There is something more, though, that trusting Jesus has done for me. Jesus forgiving me is one thing (that is, him being Saviour), but the Bible says Jesus needs to be Lord (to be boss/in charge). There was something still hanging over me that I was not sure I could let go of – the rapist.

For me, becoming a Christian means Jesus is in charge, and for Jesus to rule my life meant me forgiving the guy who raped me that evening of the party. I wish I could say this has been easy, but that would be lying. In some ways every day is a struggle, and I'm still dealing with it. It took me over four years to tell anybody what had happened, my mum included. But it has slowly become less painful to talk about and I have started dealing with it (and the thought of the rapist himself) in a much better way. It's just an amazing feeling, being able to forgive him and trust God. Jesus is in control of my whole life – even the bits that I hate. God has a plan for me.

My life has changed so drastically since the day I became a Christian. I am now playing for Reading Ladies first team, who as I write this are about to get promoted to National League division one, and God has put me in the perfect place to tell people about him and about the good news he brings. I never play a match or train without my 'audience of one' wristband, something that reminds me who I am playing for and what he's done for me. This wristband is an initiative by Christians in Sport; the band is worn by many Christian sportspeople and reminds them that whether there are thousands watching in the stands, or just a few, the only audience that matters is Jesus – and how he sees us, forgiven or unforgiven.

It was hard work plucking up the courage to tell my friends and teammates I had become a Christian, but I eventually did and they all know now. God through the Holy Spirit helps us to tell people about Jesus – I can testify that this is true. Some of them don't know what to make of it all, but others want to know more and ask all sorts of questions. To be honest, I often don't have a clue what many of the answers are, but we have been able to have some deep but fun discussions about God and Christianity.

Even though life is still extremely hard a lot of the time, and often things happen that I really don't understand, I do not blame God. I have put my complete trust in him; he created me and he knows what's best for me. Even though I often mess up, I'm trying to live my life for God. He is so fulfilling. I know what I am living for, and whatever happens in this life it is nothing compared to the certainty of heaven to come.

CHAPTER 8

MARK MORELAND HOCKEY

I guess to a certain extent I was always a sportsman. From a very early age I would be kicking a ball or holding a bat trying to hit things – not always successfully. My dad has always been very sporty and so it was probably natural that growing up I would follow suit. My earliest memories are of starting primary school and starting to play football at break and lunchtimes with my friends. I used to arrive home with my uniform covered in mud, much to my mum's despair.

Football was always my favourite sport, and although I grew up in Belfast, Manchester United was my team of choice. Like many young supporters at the time, Eric Cantona was my idol. When I got older, I went from kicking a ball around in a playground to playing for my school teams. My first memory of a proper competitive game was when I was 10 and we played against another school in a cup match. The weather was awful – we just kicked the ball from puddle to puddle. As if it wasn't bad enough that twenty-two 10-year-old boys were soaking wet and cold, the game went to extra time, and penalties. In the end we won, though.

When I got to secondary school, football was not on the list of school sports so I had to choose between rugby and hockey. Being built in such a way that a good gust of wind would carry me the full length of a playing field, I chose to play hockey, which was a lot less physically demanding. My dad used to play hockey, so I suppose I already had a bit of interest in it because of that, but the more I got into it the more I really started to enjoy it.

For the first few years I was probably below average in comparison to my peers, but I always tried my best and worked hard. I was very privileged to have some of the best coaches in my younger years to teach me the essential basics correctly, and to be involved in training camps which really improved my game. I realised that if I pushed myself I could go further than I'd ever thought I could.

At 15 I started playing senior hockey. I was up against adults, and the game got a whole lot more physical, which took me a long time to get used to. I started out playing for my club's fifth XI and managed to work my way up through the teams so that by the age of 17 I had a regular place in my club's first XI. I played alongside some of the country's top talent, some of whom are now full Irish internationals. Our team saw much success locally and also on tour to Barcelona, Berlin, and a tournament in Taunton, Somerset. Our best season was when I was 16 and playing for the school first XI. We were Irish Schools champions and won both of our local cups while boasting a whole season without a loss. I learned a lot, playing with top-class players and at a level that was a real challenge to me. I was fortunate enough to be selected to play for my province at under-18 level and again at under-21 level. I was so proud and excited to play in the Irish interprovincial tournament – in Ireland this tournament is hugely competitive.

I played for my club and my university, and was on the team three years running for the intervarsity tournament. During this time, I was selected onto the full men's provincial training squad in which we had a session taken by Mark Knowles and Jamie Dwyer, who are both Olympic gold medal winners with Australia. Mark has been World Young Player of the Year, and Jamie has been World Player of the Year four times, so it was a huge honour to be coached by these two guys who were at the very top of their game. In my final year I was selected for the Northern Ireland team which would play in the British university games in Edinburgh. For the 2010-11 season I was honoured to be the first XI captain at my provincial club. From the age of 11, I would watch the first XI and think about how great it would be to be able to play for them, not knowing that ten years on I would be the captain. Not bad at all for someone who thought he'd never make the grade.

I've been a Christian since I was young, but I wouldn't say I find it easy being a Christian in sport. Actually, it's hardest when I'm on the pitch. I grew up with a church background – both my parents were Christians – so it was normal to me, and even at primary school most people didn't find the fact that I went to church strange. I became a Christian when I was 6. I'd been to a children's mission in our church and the speaker said something that stuck with me. He said if I had died that night and I wasn't a Christian, I wouldn't go to heaven. Even at that early age I didn't feel right about this, and so lying in my bed that night I just said a simple prayer to God asking for forgiveness for all the things I'd done wrong.

I wouldn't say I'd never struggled, though. At secondary school, everything started to change. There were opportunities to try new things. Mostly it wasn't an issue – I'm fairly straight-talking and know my own mind, so I didn't find it difficult to say no to most of them. I wouldn't say I turned my back on my faith, but the best way I can explain it is that I had Sunday as my Christian day, and for the rest of the week I just did what I wanted. Having said that, I wasn't a bad kid who got into trouble; I was just not living the Christian life as I should have. I was effectively leading a double life. The turning point came when I went on a youth weekend at the age of 17 and I realised from a sermon on the first night that sitting on the fence was not an option. From then on I resolved to live out my faith fully. Several years on I can truly say that it was the best choice that I have made. I know that through all the good and the bad times, I have God to turn to.

As I said before, being a Christian in sport is not easy. When passion, emotion and commitment are combined in a team sport, let's just say that not everything is in the spirit of good sportsmanship. The topics of conversation and the language aren't exactly what you would read in the Bible. I just try my best to stay away from it as much as possible, and when an opportunity arises, I start a conversation on a subject that is acceptable.

By nature, I'm a very competitive person, so I'm not a big fan of losing. This desire to win doesn't always bring out the best in me, and it's something I'm constantly working on. Being a Christian in sport doesn't mean you just wimp out; you still get stuck in but try to stay within the constraints of the rules. One player that I really look up to is a minister – he's not only a fine hockey player, but the way he conducts himself on the pitch is something that I really admire.

Away from the pitch, you're often stuck in a car or a bus for a few hours on the way to a game, and it's then that I've found the guys generally have an interest in what I've got to say about Christianity. We have that bond that comes from being a team and being willing to work together to get a result, and the respect and camaraderie exists off the pitch as well. While most of my teammates aren't Christians, they respect my faith.

I believe my faith has made me a better sportsman. Trying to play the game in a way that honours God has an impact on the decisions that I make during play – for example, instead of trying to hit the guy who took a cheap shot at me earlier, I'm concentrating on trying to get the ball into the back of the net as many times as possible.

Many people think that being a Christian means giving everything up. In fact, it means living life to the full, for God, in the knowledge of what he has done for us. John 10:10 says that we are to live life and live it more abundantly. I am living life and playing hockey, and my faith helps me to enjoy it more than I ever have, because I know that I am glorifying God by using the gift for sport that he has given me.

CHAPTER 9

VINNY COMMONS FOOTBALL

As a child, Vinny Commons dreamt of being a professional footballer. 'I had five brothers and six sisters, and my older brothers were all very sporty. Looking up to them as I did, it's easy to see how I was drawn into sport myself. I probably spent most of my childhood on the big field next to the house, often by myself, just kicking a ball against a wall and dreaming of being a professional footballer one day. My mates would gather there too, and most nights there'd be 20 or 25 kids playing a match there.'

By the time Vinny was 11, he was invited to join the Sacred Heart team, which was run by the local Catholic priest. 'I played in the under-12s team, and after three games I'd scored nine goals, so they put me on Radio Lancashire. The local scouts heard it and came to watch me play, and I was selected for the district team under-13s. I was asked to play for them against Blackpool, on Blackpool's own ground, and the scouts at Blackpool saw me and asked me to try out for them. I went from Blackpool to Bradford City, and by the time I was 17 I was playing for the youth team at Manchester City.'

Vinny was living his dream, though he preferred Manchester United to Man. City. 'Of course I couldn't go to matches and support Man. U because I was always playing when they were – but it was still great to be playing for Man. City.' By the time he was 19 he'd passed his A levels, and went to Manchester to train as a sports teacher.

At home, though, things weren't so good. 'Some members of my family were struggling with alcohol, and through that my eldest sister became a Christian at university in Liverpool. I was brought up in a Catholic church where all the services were in Latin, which of course I didn't understand. I felt as though I was living my dream, being at Man. City, but as I actually achieved my ambition of becoming a footballer, I realised that I still felt empty, and I didn't know what would fill that void in my heart.'

Vinny believed that part of this feeling that something was missing stemmed from something that had happened when he was 15. 'I used to do a milk round – which was tremendous for football training, because it was basically two hours of running around – and one of the other boys on the round was killed in a motorbike accident on his birthday. I was really shaken by it. He was just two years older than me, and I didn't have any answers about what happened when someone died – and what was going to happen to me when I died. I asked everyone, and all I got was silence. No one had any answers for me.'

At 19, Vinny still didn't have any answers, and so he started talking to Angela and Philomena, two of his sisters who had become Christians. 'Phil said to me "Vinny, salvation is a gift; a gift from God." I argued that it wasn't a gift, you had to be good. I couldn't conceive of a Christianity where you didn't have to uphold your side of the bargain and be good, because God was good; so for someone to say it was free, I thought that was too easy. I couldn't understand how you could be saved, just like that.'

During his first year in Manchester, Vinny was still searching. 'I knew there was a God – I'd seen the change in my family, in Angela, Phil, and now in my other sister Carmel – and yet I still didn't have any answers to the problem of what happens when a person dies.' But that year, Vinny was to have an encounter with Christ that would change his life completely.

'I met a lad at a youth club at the end of my first term and he asked me to come to a youth meeting the following Sunday. I said I'd go, and I did, but if I'm honest, I thought these people were all strange. The meeting was a bit extreme for me – they were charismatics so there were people speaking in tongues (see Acts 2:1–13; 1 Cor. 14) and falling over, which seemed very odd to me – and so I was looking for a way to get out. In the end I told a lie. I said I rang my mother every Sunday, and so I'd have to go or she'd worry. As I walked back up the lane to my accommodation, I decided that I would have to put God out of my mind. If I did that, I thought, I'd be normal, just like everyone else on campus, and I'd be able to get on with my life. In need of distraction, I went to the gym, because all the basketball players gathered there on Sunday nights. We had the national basketball coach on campus, so basketball was a big thing at Manchester. But no one was there. I thought maybe they'd gone on a pub crawl or something ... So I went back to my room and, still looking for a distraction, I turned the TV on. There was a programme about the devil, and I only watched about three minutes of it before I had to turn it off, really frightened. I started to think that maybe there was a devil, and maybe there was a God, and a heaven and a hell. I couldn't find any peace. I tried to pray and it felt as though the sky was a canopy of brass, cutting me off from whatever was beyond me, and I felt utterly separated from God. I was terrified, because I knew I'd done wrong, and I wasn't sure I was going to heaven. The thought of going to hell terrified me. I got so frightened I began to shake, and I sat down on my bed. I'd had two years of turmoil, two years of trying to find God, and all that effort went into a prayer. I cried out, 'God, if you are here and you can forgive me, please come and live in my heart.' I threw myself onto what I thought was nothing, I committed my life not knowing if there was anyone there, and as I did, it dawned on me that I'd come right to the end of myself, and it was there that I found the beginning of God. By his Holy Spirit, Jesus came into my heart. It was like a shaft of light – I didn't see anything, but I felt peace.'

Despite his conversion, Vinny still had questions about his new faith. 'I really struggled to trust God. In the church I was brought up in, you could never say you were sure of heaven; that is the sin of presumption. You have to do good works. I just couldn't understand how I could trust this God who I couldn't see, when I couldn't trust people. I knew I couldn't trust people because I'd seen they all had the ability to do wrong. My sister Angela said, "Concentrate on the cross where Jesus died and you will see it." She told me to ask for assurance from God for forgiveness and heaven. So I prayed, but I kept thinking about the cross, and what it meant. Then one day I was in my room and my post arrived. The minister of a church in Birmingham had written to me, and he said, "Vincent, your experience is like that of John Bunyan." Well, I didn't even know who John Bunyan was! Underneath that he'd written "Jn. 6:37. All those the Father gives me will come to me and whoever comes to me I'll never drive away." I found later that this was the verse that helped Bunyan become a Christian. At the end of the letter he wrote, "Have you ever come to Jesus and asked him?" and I thought, "Yes, I did on Sunday" and then he had written, "Therefore you're in. No one is cast out." Then I knew I was sure of heaven as I'd come to him, and anyone who comes must get in, because he can't cast them out. That's how I got full assurance of faith, because Jesus died for me on the cross, and bore the crown of thorns for my sins. That was a fact that could not be altered.'

Vinny says, 'For the next few days it wasn't just about knowing God's forgiveness in my heart, it was understanding that my life was no longer my own. I had to be broken to a point where I could give in to God. When I gave in, that's when I felt real peace. And giving in to God had a bearing on my sport.'

The Manchester college team had done well, winning the British Colleges two years running, and Vinny was due to be skipper in his second year. However, he says, 'My challenge was that football had a claim on too much of my heart. I'd lived for football and now God was saying, "Look, Vinny, now you're mine, football has to be your servant, not your master."'

Vinny was playing semi-professionally at the time, and when he graduated, he worked for the Manpower Services Commission, and then landed a job in a school in London's East End, through a Christian PE teacher he knew. He worked at the school for a while, and then they sent him to do a course with the FA, where he was asked to play for Grays Athletic FC. 'I played for Grays first team, and the first time I got to the ground for training the coach told me to do a few laps of the pitch. When I got to the far end he was waiting for me and asked me what I was doing, shouting that he'd told me to do sit-ups instead. In fact, the coach and his brother ran the club, and they were identical twins. They played the same trick on all the new lads. I was there for a year and a half and then I got another job as head of PE at a school in Southport. That was really when I started to move away from football and got more involved in Christian work. I left my footballer's life behind, and started to take Christian outreach more seriously.'

When Vinny was later made redundant from his job at the school, he wrote to Manchester City, Liverpool, Everton and Preston, asking for work. 'Gary Peters at Preston North End asked me to come for an interview for a job coaching boys, and he offered me the post. I said, "It's a conviction of mine not to play on a Sunday." He looked at me and said, "Are you telling us that we're offering you a job at a professional football club and you're turning it down because you won't turn up on a Sunday?" I'd prayed about the interview beforehand, and I said, "Yeah, I am." He said, "OK, we'll take you on that basis," and I worked for them for ten years, developing football players.'

In January 2011 Vinny left Preston. He's heavily involved in Christian outreach, running soccer clinics and Christian sports camps. 'I've run a sports camp for sixteen years that I founded – 100 kids and fifty staff come every year to that, and people also ask me to coach their kids. In terms of what I'm doing next, Man. City have just asked me to send them my CV, so I may end up coaching there. I still play, too – I was selected for the Liverpool over-50s team. I was going to play centre-half and then they put me centre midfield because I can still run fast, and now I'm centre-forward. After my first game I was top scorer ... but I walked off the pitch with two torn hamstrings – it was agony.'

Football was once everything to Vinny Commons; now it's a way that Vinny can share his faith. 'Football is a way of reaching kids who just want to come and do a bit of sport, and hear about the gospel. I work as an evangelist, sharing the gospel and trying to make it relevant, and somehow God takes hold of it and uses it. Now, rather than feeling like the aim of my life is to be a footballer, I've dedicated my life to God.'

CHAPTER 10

GAIL JAMES JAVELIN

I was always very into sport. If there was a club on in school I wanted to join it – it didn't matter what sport it was, I would always have a go.

I threw the javelin for the first time at my secondary school sports day. My teacher stood on the school record line, her notebook ready, and then watched the javelin fly over her head! I remember everyone was very impressed when that happened, but they said, 'Well, that's sporty Gail for you.' I suppose they didn't think it was so unusual. The following summer, though, things were different because there was a new teacher at school who used to drink in the pub with Steve Cram's coach, Jimmy Hedley, and between them they ended up putting me in touch with the man who would go on to coach me, Carl Johnson.

I went up to Gateshead Stadium and met Carl, and he shook his head, saying, 'It's going to take a long time, you're uncoordinated and you're too tall for your body.'

(That's a north-east expression – it meant I had grown quickly and was gangly and awkward.) That's the sort of encouraging thing that coaches tend to say! He had a point, though; at 13 I was already the height I am today: 6 ft. Anyway, I can't have been that bad because he agreed to coach me, and I started training at the stadium.

My first year of competition was the year I was 14, and in that year I came second in the English School Championships. I really came out of nowhere. I wasn't concentrating on javelin exclusively, I also played County tennis and County netball. In fact, when I got married, my dad's quote at my wedding was, 'Gail's sisters got tired just watching her.' I never stopped. But my athletics really became the main thing I did. I threw discus and javelin. I threw for the County and for the North of England, and then I went on to throw for the British senior team four times when I was 18. At the end of that season, I was just a metre and a half short of the Olympic qualifying distance for Barcelona 1992.

Everything was looking promising, then I went to college in Crewe. I was dreadfully homesick. I missed my family, my friends, my coach and the whole sporting environment. Then I got sick with a glandular fever-type illness that meant I couldn't train. When I left home, my training was the only thing in my life that was going to stay the same, and I really needed that stability, so to have that taken away from me hit me hard. The Athletics Board sent me down to Harley Street for testing, and the doctors came up with a diagnosis of a virus. They told me that

I'd need regular testing for three to four years and that this was going to be a long-term illness. I ended up quite low and depressed, looking for some answers as to why everything had gone so wrong.

I used to lie in bed on campus on Sunday mornings and hear church bells ringing, and I ended up walking into a church a couple of times. I should say that although I was sent to Sunday school as a child, my parents had no religious views whatsoever. They just sent my sisters and me to Sunday school because that's what middle-class children are supposed to do. Anyway, although I'd been to Sunday school, I obviously hadn't been paying attention, because when I went to one of these services I spotted an advert for a gospel meeting and I thought that meant a black gospel choir! I went along to hear it, and instead of a choir there was a guy at the front preaching the gospel instead. He said that Jesus had died to take away my sins, he'd died for me, and taken away my mistakes, because he was perfect. I don't think I really thought much about God until then. I hadn't even associated church with being a place where God might be! But once I heard what the preacher had to say, I accepted Jesus as Lord, and I gave my life to him.

I was due to go out to the States on a four-year sports scholarship and Masters degree, but I felt very strongly that God was telling me to stay in the UK and work with children. I also felt that he wanted me to give up athletics. So I did. Since then, I've had the privilege of working both with churches in the UK, and on short term missions to

Europe and Africa, alongside my husband and our two children, teaching kids about God.

When I became a Christian, my parents found it very difficult. They were, and are, atheists, and they were convinced that I was saying they weren't good enough, that they weren't enough to make me happy. In fact, I had a fantastic childhood. My parents were amazing – they were the most supportive family anyone could ever ask for. You know those Dad's Taxi stickers? My dad must have earned about a hundred – he used to ferry me everywhere, all of the time. My mum cooked a special diet for me; they just did everything, they were brilliant. What they couldn't understand, and what they still can't really understand, is that the gap in my life was God-shaped. Nothing and no one else could fill it.

When I gave up athletics I was 19 and still at college. My decision not to carry on my sport came as a huge shock. Also, it was difficult for them because my sport was part of the family identity by then. I'm from the north-east, and in the Geordie culture sport is everything. I was in the *South Shields Gazette* every week, and the whole town knew me, and was proud of me. I'd get the bus to training with my javelin in a drainpipe as that was the only way I could safely transport it, and I'd have to stand by the stairs because it was the only place with enough room for the pipe, and everyone would say to me as they passed, 'Have a good training session, Gail!'

When I walked away from sport, I didn't live at home any more, but my parents were still part of our community. They'd have people coming up to them on the street and asking, 'How's Gail doing? She hasn't been in the paper for a while.' For them to have to tell people that I'd given all that up because I was a Christian now, when they didn't understand my decision themselves, must have been very tough.

My sport kept me on the straight and narrow through my teenage years. I wasn't out drinking or getting into trouble because I was always training, and it gave me great discipline. It was a fantastic start in life for me, and I am very thankful for it. I met some lovely people, from big name sportspeople to my wonderful coach. Athletics was, and is to some extent, still pretty much an amateur sport. My coach was paid as a national coach for work he did with the British team, and yet he was willing to give up his time to come and train me two or three nights a week. It's amazing that there are people like that who are so willing to do so much for young people, and he definitely inspired me in my own work with children. I don't regret any of the time I spent on my sport, and I don't regret giving it up, either. Sport was my god, but now I have found the true and living God.

CHAPTER 11

DEREK JEFFERSON FOOTBALL

I was born in the north-east of England in 1948, and played football for school and county. Ipswich Town Football Club asked me to sign to them when I was 16, and I spent seventeen years playing football at the top level for Ipswich Town, Wolves, and Hereford, as well as two years in America. I played alongside national and international stars, and for famous managers including Bobby Robson. If I had to pick two highlights, I'd say one would be getting promotion from the second to the first division with Ipswich Town, and the other would be getting the chance to play against Pelé – probably the best football player ever – when I was in America.

So life was good to me, but then tragedy struck. While I was playing for Wolverhampton Wanderers, I lost my 2-year-old daughter, Victoria, very suddenly. I'd been to Sunday school when I was young, and it hadn't made much sense to me, but after Victoria's death I was immediately convinced that there could not possibly be a loving God.

I started to drink heavily, trying to fill the emptiness, and a while later my marriage broke down. I didn't understand it at the time, but much of the lifestyle I was living was my way of trying to cope with the grief I felt. It was while visiting my parents in Middlesbrough just after my marriage failed that I attended a church service, which was to change my life completely. During the service a young man explained how God had changed his life. He talked about Jesus as a real person and of the forgiveness of God that he had experienced. I found myself crying. I wanted what he had. I needed a new start. I had never really had any peace in my life and that night I found a peace I had not known before. It has stayed with me ever since.

I was still playing football, but I qualified as a football coach in the hope that when my career came to an end I could still be involved in football. When I did stop playing, I went on to be appointed reserve team manager at Birmingham City under Jim Smith. My life took on a new dimension. I was involved in football at the highest level, but had a sense of peace and purpose I had never had before. Around this time I got married again, to Linda, the daughter of a minister, and we now have six children between us, including two from my previous marriage.

Working at Birmingham City was great. I was a Christian then and enjoyed working with players on a daily basis, helping them improve and become better players. In total, I was at Birmingham City for five years. I was attending a local church and came to the conclusion after a period of time that God was leading me in another direction. After praying about it for six months, I left football to take a position working for a drug company. I had no formal qualifications, and it just so happened that at my interview the sales manager turned out to be a Newcastle United supporter. Being from the north-east, I obviously support Newcastle too. I had to go through several tests to see if I fitted into their profile but eventually got the job.

I worked in the drug industry for eight years, but then I came to believe that God wanted me to return to football. I had this conviction that I needed to be giving something back to the community in a more direct way. This was about ten years ago. I felt God wanted me to use my football skills to help reach young people with the Christian message – I wanted to 'put something back into the game' and pass on what I had learned to youngsters, but with an added dimension. Through my own faith experiences I became convinced that coaching youngsters the right way in football, based on Christian principles, could help with life skills including self-discipline, self-esteem, sportsmanship and team spirit. It would also help to bridge the gap between church and community in a positive way.

I talked it over with my minister, and that summer Sports Pursuits was born. A group of youngsters came together for three days of intensive training. Important football skills, life skills and disciplines together with Christian teaching formed the basis of the course. At the end of the three days there was a medal and certificate presentation at the church with 300 parents attending – over 80 per cent of them had no experience of church outside this.

Today, Sports Pursuits is a charity that counts some well-known personalities in the sports world as trustees and members of the Council of Reference. It is now a rapidly expanding organisation, which encompasses a variety of sports and a growing number of Christian coaches. Our vision is to bring a Christian message and ethos to all youngsters (but especially those with social disadvantage) by making high-quality sporting opportunities available. I firmly believe that if God asks you to give something up he replaces it with something better. I gave up football, but now help youngsters to enjoy sport and improve their skills. I also show them how being a Christian can help them to enjoy it even more.

CHAPTER 12

DANNY SITTON TENNIS

Like most people, I guess, I love my mum and dad very much. They have been great to me. They love me unconditionally and are always very supportive of what I want to do and achieve in life. Despite their partnership and agreement in this, as I grew up, there was something quite different about the two of them: Mum was a Christian and Dad wasn't. Though Dad never opposed or stopped Mum from believing what she did, it wasn't for him.

I guess it was my mum's beliefs that rubbed off on me the most, though, and although I can't pinpoint precisely when I became a Christian, it was sometime during the visit of the American evangelist Billy Graham to London in the late 1980s. Though there was nothing dramatic about my 'conversion', I did become incredibly excited about reading the Bible.

Just a few years later, though, my spiritual life got derailed. A pivotal moment of my life was approaching. I had become involved in a youth group at my local Baptist church in London. I was working for the Metropolitan Police Service at the time and enjoying life and all that it threw at me. The Met was hard work; sometimes harrowing, but fun and rewarding at the same time. Surprisingly, though, it was in the church that my problems arose.

I started a relationship with a lady in the church; a married lady. It completely crippled my spiritual life. I didn't know what I believed any longer. Deep down I knew the truth of Jesus, who he is and what he has done – and yet in my day-to-day life, I was living a lie. All I was interested in was chasing after my desires, with a married woman. I stopped talking to my friends about my Christian beliefs, I took no enjoyment in church and spending time with church friends. I'd abandoned my moral code, and I thought nothing of whether my affair was right or wrong. It was fun, exhilarating, passionate and enjoyable. I was living for myself and it was great – on the surface.

Some time later the relationship came to an end, but even when it was over, the guilt of what I had done and the hypocrisy of telling others I was a Christian ate away at me. This continued for the best part of ten years. I couldn't shake off the past. I had totally messed up. I claimed to be a Christian and yet I was the worst example out there. What on earth was going on and how could I put it right?

I had been in the Met for a while, but had always wanted to coach tennis. The financial risk was high, but

I desperately wanted to give it a go. I went for it, and very quickly (thankfully) it proved a good move. I had played tennis to a reasonable but not exceptional level, and I greatly enjoyed this new career. I still attended church to satisfy my deep-down acknowledgement of and agreement with the Christian faith, but found it very difficult during the week to live as someone who believed it. I had a string of relationships with non-Christian girls, and even the relationships I had with Christian girls weren't particularly pleasing to God. I was doing stuff with them that I should not have done, and my spiritual life was still quite dysfunctional. Looking back, perhaps I had got a taste for it following the affair, and now I just couldn't get back on my feet in a Christian way. I didn't feel I deserved to call myself a Christian because of the example I'd set. I wasn't living as God tells Christians to live. I was blatantly disobeying him. Was I even a Christian, I wondered?

At the time I was semi-conscious of this spiritual battle in my life, but didn't seem able to do anything about it. This was made even worse by my new role as a head coach at a good tennis club – an environment where temptation seemed to be around every corner. I was doing a job I loved in a wealthy area of London, surrounded by hot women in tennis gear. It was probably a great opportunity to tell people about Jesus, but I didn't. I was still too absorbed with myself, and what pleasure I could have in life.

Strangely, I would still read the Bible every day. I had lots of academic knowledge about Christianity and used to have great debates with clients about various topical issues to do with Christianity. However, all my learning and my ability to quote the Bible had no impact on who I was and how I lived. It was like knowing exactly how to drive, but never getting in a car to do so. I knew what Jesus had done for me, and how I needed to respond. I needed him to be boss of my life to demonstrate that he, not I, was in charge. But I wasn't doing it.

I had no real knowledge of Christianity in my heart. God had given me a fantastic job, doing something I loved; yet I often fell into the same sins and gave way to the same temptations. I had never ceased to believe in Jesus, but my heart was stubbornly closed because of the guilt and my perceived hypocrisy of not consistently living the Christian life.

The big turning point finally came, though quite unexpectedly. I was seeing a girl from the tennis club who wasn't a Christian, and had been doing so for around a year. I thought it was no big deal that she wasn't a Christian, especially as many of my other ex-girlfriends had also not been Christians. I guess I had often thought that I probably shouldn't marry them, but what was the harm in going out with them?

One day, for no obvious reason, I felt God clearly telling me I had to finish this relationship immediately. OK, so there was no big, booming voice, but I just sensed that God was telling me to stop things, to take it no further. It's hard to describe, and I know it sounds kind of odd, but I knew I must not wait. I did not receive a verbal message from God, but this was as good as one – it was not a vague feeling of 'I should probably finish this at some point in the future' – this was an immediate command. I had never had anything like this before – this was totally clear. I was gutted, because she was a great girl. I was very keen on her and reluctant to break it off. For some reason, maybe through fear, I was obedient to what God was saying, and broke it off, straightaway. It was the hardest thing to explain to her (I don't think I explained it very well), but I ended it whilst wondering why all this had just happened.

I can't explain it, but I want to make clear: this was not just me doing the right thing – God specifically commanded me to do this. Over the years, when I had been doing other things that I shouldn't have been, I had always known deep down that my actions were not pleasing God, but I just drifted along and circumstances would often bring me out of situations. On this occasion, things were somehow different.

After the break-up, as the weeks passed, I continued to work as normal. However, things were different in another area of my life. I had a power I can't explain, but spiritually I was a new person. God completely renewed me – it was like a massive weight had been taken from around my neck. I had a lot of confessing to do and lots of forgiveness to seek, but for the first time in ten years I genuinely felt forgiven. Words cannot adequately describe this – God literally cleaned away all the spiritual damage I had done to my relationship with him. I could look people in the eye and talk about Christianity for the first time in ages. There were some big changes. I made a commitment to God that I would never date a girl who was not a Christian, and also a commitment that I would not give in to the temptation to sleep with them before marriage. There were some little changes, too: I changed the music I listened to because I suddenly thought some of the language was inappropriate; I made a huge effort to avoid the sin of lust, as well as many other things. I honestly didn't know how I'd be able to change, but the funny thing is that once I handed all this over to God, it was made so easy for me. Suddenly I found that my thoughts were pure, I didn't want to listen to music that I shouldn't or watch TV programmes that were ungodly. I no longer checked girls out and mentally undressed them. Everything about me changed and this was not done through my strength but through God's strength. Like I say, I can't explain it, unless I put it down to God.

I honestly believe that all God asked me to do was one thing – to end a relationship that I shouldn't have been having in the first place. I took one small step of obedience and God showered me with blessings in so many areas of my life. I'm not saying I'm perfect by any means, but God has totally renewed me. I look back over the last ten years and realise that I wasted so much time I could have used for God's purposes. I had one foot in this world and the other foot in my Christian world, and the two just didn't mix. With relationships, I have come to learn that as a Christian, if your partner does not bring you closer to God and enrich your spiritual life then they will drag you away from God instead. There is no such thing as neutral ground in your walk with God – either you're going forward in your spiritual life or you're going backwards ... you're never in the middle. I quickly came to realise how unwise it was to enter into a relationship where your partner is not a believer. How can you possibly have God at the centre of and as the focal part of your lives and your relationship if one of you is not a Christian?

I have always been really blessed by God in my role as a tennis coach. I am now a qualified performance tennis coach and God has brought lots of talented players to my club. I really don't think I'm a particularly brilliant coach – I just believe that if you leave your own abilities in God's hands, things turn out well.

A little after God renewed my Christian life I started dating a girl called Angelene, from the church I attend. I am so grateful to God for bringing her into my life, and pleased to say we are now married with two daughters. Looking back, God had everything totally in control. Had I not been obedient when he told me to finish the previous relationship, I have no doubt that God would not have rewarded me by bringing such a wonderful woman into my life. God cleared out so much sin and is transforming me into the guy he wants. I am not perfect, but I am forgiven, and God is changing me every day to become more like him.

CHAPTER 13

JONATHAN STOBBS FENCING

As a 9-year-old, the first time I tried fencing my head was full of the Three Musketeers, Robin Hood and the other swashbuckling heroes I wanted to emulate. However, I would soon learn that modern fencing is very different to the swordplay I saw on the silver screen.

My dad used to fence, and so he'd taken me to a club at the local YMCA in Southport to try it, hoping that it would be something we could do together. I can remember the little YMCA room very clearly. The ceiling was so low that you could not do certain moves without dragging the point of the sword along it. However, on those Thursday nights I grew to really enjoy the sessions: the coaching, the sparring matches, and then the competitions. I was fortunate to be at a club that was willing to give young fencers a chance, certainly in local league competitions. I can remember visiting various venues on week nights, facing big adult fencers from other clubs, and feeling nervous, but also excited at the challenge. There were some bruising encounters in those league competitions, but it only whetted my appetite for more.

Modern fencing is mentally and physically challenging; some have said it is like chess with swords. You have to be physically able to endure quick bursts of energy and speed, as well as sustain momentum in those times when opponents are figuring each other out. The key is to be able to out-think your opponent with tactics, speed, agility, and accuracy. The point of fencing is to place a hit on your opponent without being hit, as though your life depended on it – in times of duelling, it did.

As I continued to train and to fence competitively, I also began to attend other local clubs on different nights to enhance my training. We used to go to Formby Ravens Fencing Club, West Lancashire Fencing Club, and on occasion the Dolphin Fencing Club at Crosby. With the support of my mum and dad, fencing became a major part of my life. Obviously, with the success that I began to experience in local, national, and then international competitions, the momentum carried me onwards. I will never forget the encouragement I received in those early years from my family, but also from some of the lovely people in those clubs who were so committed to the sport at that local level.

I began to compete in competitions as a foil fencer, and won a number of local and regional titles in that discipline. However, the discipline that became my favourite, and the concentration of all my training, was épée. This is the weapon that targets all of the body, and is the closest to duelling that safety regulations will allow.

I trained at a local level for a while. However, as I progressed in competitions, although my dad was my main coach, I still had to travel to various parts of the country for specific training with specialised coaches. So I would go to Manchester, Durham, and sometimes the London area for both regional and national training sessions and days. The training was intense physically, and then following that there would also be specific épée training during individual lessons. I was also privileged to attend a training camp in France. It was a real eye-opener to the differences in approach between France and Britain – although things are beginning to change.

I saw success quite early on, winning a large number of regional events such as Lancashire Schools and Cheshire Schools. I also represented the North-West Regional Team at both cadet (under-17) and senior level. I won and was placed regularly in the top three in a number of national events in both the under-17 and under-20 series that were held around the country.

I also began to compete in the Men's National Opens at the age of 13, which again took place around the country, and began to rise in the rankings to a top twenty position. Alongside this, my ranking in Great Britain under-17 and under-20 lists would regularly be in the top five, and for a period of time I was ranked number one in the country for both age categories. I was part of a group of fencers that went to Aalborg, Denmark in 1996 for the International

Centennial Youth Games, where I was part of an épée team that won the bronze medal against other teams such as Norway, Denmark, Holland, Germany, and so on.

When I was still very young for the categories, I was privileged to be selected to represent Great Britain at Junior (under-20) World Cup events. It was an incredible feeling to be called up for the national team that very first time. I would then travel regularly around Europe to competitions with the GB squad. The standard was superb, and it took a while to adjust, but over time I began to adapt to the circumstances and the pressure.

I had the honour of captaining the England épée team in the Junior Home International against Scotland, Wales and Northern Ireland. We were undefeated. I also competed at university – being placed in the top eight in the British University Sports Association Épée Tournament in 2002, and captaining the Royal Holloway Fencing Squad for two of my three years there. I was awarded full colours from Royal Holloway, and half-colours from the University of London.

However, by the time I got to university, all wasn't well. I had already begun to experience some major problems with my knee which meant that I had taken a step back from the intensity of national and international competitions that I had known in the years before. During a national training session, I began to feel sharp discomfort in my right knee, only for it then to start locking. Imagine being in the middle of a fight and then your knee locks and you cannot put any weight on it – a recipe for disaster. I had a series of X-rays and scans, and then a knee arthroscopy. I had some issues with floating cartilage, and other weaknesses in my knee, and though the surgery was at first thought to have been successful, it soon became apparent that the issue was not resolved. I could no longer rely on my body not to let me down, and it became clear that continuing in my sport at the level I was competing was becoming increasingly difficult. It seemed that the Lord had other plans for me.

I was privileged to be brought up in a Christian home, and was consequently taken to church from a very young age. However, despite these influences, the Lord Jesus Christ and what it means to follow him wasn't something I knew personally until I was 11. I knew the facts of what it meant to be a Christian, I knew Bible verses as I'd been to Sunday school, and I wouldn't say I was opposed to the idea, but it just wasn't real to me. Yet, when I was 11, I was in an evening service at my home church, Grace Baptist in Southport. The preacher was pastor Peter Day, and that night he vividly spoke on the reality of heaven and hell. I knew that without Jesus I had no hope in this life or the next. He spoke of sin; how my sin made me at war with God, and there was nothing I could do to change that. He said that the Bible made it clear there was nothing I could do to make myself right with God. Thankfully, he also spoke of the Saviour, the One who had come, who had died for sinners like me on the cross at Calvary, and that by his death as substitute, my sins could be forgiven and I could be made right with God. To be forgiven I had to acknowledge my sin, repent, and trust in Christ.

That night I went home, and in my bedroom prayed a simple prayer to ask for forgiveness, and to trust wholly in Christ to save me and keep me. For the very first time, it was not just facts or something that I had heard, it was real, and while nothing dramatic happened, I knew I was forgiven. The fact that Jesus loved me, and gave himself for me, that he shed his blood to atone, to deal with my sin, and to wash me clean, overwhelmed me. Not only that, but I realised that the forgiveness and deliverance that was now mine was purely born of grace – it was a free gift. I did not deserve it, but God in his love and kindness saved me. He changed me, and the purpose of my life became to live for him.

Being a Christian made a massive difference to the way that I approached sport. My purpose was to do all things to the glory of God, and that included training, competing, and the way that I conducted myself in those situations. I am a very competitive person, and that can be a major fault, certainly in my attitude towards others, but being a Christian and relying upon the Lord helped me to bring those tendencies under control. Of course, it didn't mean that I didn't mess up on occasion, but my approach was different from the vast majority of those around me. I wanted to be a strong competitor, but gracious, and someone who was not known as arrogant, but approachable and kind. I prayed at the beginning and throughout every competition that the Lord would help me to honour him, no matter what the outcome. I remember watching *Chariots of Fire*, and really identifying with the moment when Eric Liddell explains that he believed that God made him fast, and when he ran he felt God's pleasure. There were times when I was using all the ability and skill that God had given me in this area, and at the same time knowing a sense of peace, joy and exhilaration that is hard to put into words.

I made sure that I read my Bible daily, and ensured I had time alone with the Lord. It was often hard travelling so much, and being away from church and fellowship – it was easy to become lonely. But I found that God's promises were real, and that he would be there with me in every circumstance. Being away from home at an early age presented some huge tests spiritually, but the Lord preserved me, and while it wasn't always easy, he always gave me the grace and strength I needed to endure. This was especially true during my mid-teens when my mum was diagnosed with cancer. Continuing to compete, to travel, with the additional burden of worrying about her was very hard, but I came to understand that Christians can truly cast their burdens on the Lord, for he cares for them (see 1 Pet. 5:7). He brought my mum through her cancer, but in those months I learned much about what it meant to trust in the Lord with all my heart, and to not lean on my own understanding (see Prov. 3:5).

So when I started to experience problems with my knee, although I didn't find it easy to deal with the fact that my future plans for progressing in my sport were being taken away, I had to learn that God always has the best in store for his people. Even though I felt as though I was missing out, he gave me many blessings and opportunities that far outweighed the sporting success that I was aiming for.

In the period since leaving university, I qualified to be a secondary school history teacher. I did this for a number of years, teaching in Redruth, Cornwall. The Lord also blessed me with a Christian wife, Jenna, and three lovely children: Joel, Jemima and Joanna.

I loved teaching, but it soon became clear that the Lord again had a different path for me and my family. In January 2008, I became the pastor of Penzance Baptist Church, and it is an amazing privilege to serve the Lord where he wants me to be. I have found that many of the disciplines learned and applied through sport have helped me – for in the New Testament Paul speaks of the Christian life and Christian service in terms of running the race, or disciplined living, like an athlete, or pursuing the goal set before us (see for example 1 Cor. 9:24; Gal. 2:2; Gal. 5:7; Heb. 12:1).

Ultimately, knowing Jesus is the greatest thing we can ever have, and compared to this, sport has its brilliant moments, but nothing compares to being forgiven and right with God, brought into a real relationship with him. To know his love, his strength, his care, his guidance and his provision in every circumstance helped me to keep a balance in sport – to give my all, to pursue excellence, yet also to realise that winning is great, but it's not everything.

Of far greater importance is being right with God through his Son, Jesus Christ, and in him to know real life in all its fullness. My favourite Bible verse is Philippians 4:13, 'I can do all things through Christ who strengthens me' (NKJV). It is learning to realise that it is our utter dependence upon Christ that gives us strength to face every trial, every circumstance, knowing that he will give to his people all that they need to do that which he has for them. It is that truth and his grace which has caused, and continues to cause, me to endure, to run the race, and to press towards that eternal goal.

CHAPTER 14

JOHN GILLESPIE
AMERICAN FOOTBALL

My family moved to the USA when I was 8 years old, and so as I grew up my greatest desire was to play American football. Unfortunately, I was a skinny little kid with thick glasses! The smallest in my class, I was constantly picked on, and was the last person you'd expect to be chosen for any team sports.

By the time I was 13, though, I was desperate to fulfil my dream, and so while all the other kids were outside messing around, I was in my basement lifting weights, or out on the streets doing laps of the neighbourhood. I trained so hard that at the age of 14 I finally made my local school team, only to end up as a 'benchwarmer.' Instead of playing, I could be found waiting to be called on as a substitute. But I kept on training and training, harder than anyone I knew, and at 16 became the starting linebacker and fullback for my town's varsity team. At 17 I was elected captain of that team, and by the time I was 18, I had numerous opportunities to play for various universities in the eastern USA.

But in April of my senior year, I suffered a serious knee injury that required immediate surgery, and all my dreams of playing at university level were dashed. I remember the painful phone call I had to make to the head coach of the university I had hoped to play for, telling him that my upcoming operation would prevent me from playing any more serious football.

I made a drastic decision, and headed west to university in Ohio, to study business law. I wasn't a Christian, and I was still devastated at the loss of my promising sports career, but while my dreams of football were over, God's dreams for me were not. It was at university that I met, for the first time in my life, real followers of Jesus Christ. I was confronted with the gospel and with my own sinfulness and I became a Christian. Many of the Christians I met were actually members of the university team, and I began to study the Bible and lift weights with them. Even though I couldn't play football with them, we had a common fellowship in Jesus Christ that was much deeper than sport. Many of those players went on to play in the National Football League (NFL).

More importantly, it was at university that I met my wife-to-be, Teresa. We met at our campus Christian fellowship, and soon realised that we were to spend our lives together. Had I not suffered that knee injury, I might never have met Jesus Christ or Teresa! I believe that God was directing my life, and turning a bad event to good.

Teresa and I have been married now for thirty years, and have been blessed with seven children. God's direction for my life brought me into Christian ministry, and I have been pastoring churches for over thirty years, for the last twenty-five years in Cornwall, UK.

My love for sport has never diminished. I played and coached golf, and swam on a local team for many years, and now I am part of the coaching staff of an American football team here in Cornwall that my son plays for. Coaching is the next best thing to playing, and I can actually be involved in shaping young men's lives, helping them to develop life skills and character through the rigours of sport, endurance and training.

My greatest passion, though, is for the gospel of Jesus Christ. That God's Son would die on a cruel cross to pay for my sins, and save me from a sure and deserved hell, is the greatest victory of all.

CHAPTER 15

RICHARD LEADBEATER FOOTBALL

'The word "career" makes what I did sound quite grand. Actually, my career as a professional footballer was over by the time I was 26.' Though most young footballers dream of being the next David Beckham, the experience Richard Leadbeater had is often the reality.

'I started playing football aged 9, after my mother saw an advert in the paper for a local team,' Richard explains. He joined the team, and discovered he was good at football. So good, in fact, that aged 12 he was spotted by talent scouts for Wolverhampton Wanderers. 'They were the team I supported, so it was a big thrill.' Every Thursday for four years, Richard played with Wolves schoolboys, as well as playing with his local team. At 16, he was offered a professional contract with Wolves. 'That was the big moment for me: do I stay on at school to do A levels, or do I take the opportunity to fulfil my dream of becoming a professional footballer? Obviously, it wasn't a difficult decision.'

For two years, Richard played for Wolves and did odd jobs, everything from cleaning boots to cleaning toilets. 'It's not all glamorous!' he says. At the end of the two years, he was one of just three boys, out of hundreds of hopefuls, to be offered a full-time contract. 'For the early part of my career, I actually did even better than I was expected to. I was competing with hundreds of other people who all wanted the same thing. I was a centre-forward, and everyone wants to play centre-forward, but somehow I just kept getting through the trials and being picked for the team.'

Life as a professional footballer also seemed to live up to its promise. Richard was being paid to do something he loved, playing alongside his sporting heroes – and being part of a Championship team meant recognition. People wanted tickets, photos and autographs: what teenage boy wouldn't enjoy that?

Towards the end of Richard's second full-time year with Wolves, he was loaned to Hereford United. He scored seven goals in twelve games, and after a spell back with Wolves, he transferred to Hereford United permanently, at the age of 21. He scored a hat trick in his second game for Hereford, against local rivals Kidderminster Harriers. But after that, things didn't go quite so well.

'I just didn't live up to expectations. I'd shown a lot of early promise, but I didn't go on to fulfil my potential … the truth is that I did very well early on, and then I started to struggle. I found that hard, because I'd always been the one who got into the team, and then I wasn't.

Little things made a difference. For example, Graham Taylor was my manager at Wolves and he really liked me. Then he got the sack, slightly harshly I felt, and the new manager didn't know me ... so I didn't have that advantage any more. Leaving Wolves was tough, because it resulted in me playing semi-professionally, and playing part-time, not full-time. At a club like Wolves, you come to think of yourself in terms of being a footballer. I'd gone from playing for a famous club where fans recognised me (occasionally), to just walking down the street being me. Even though I knew that when I was with Wolves, people were interested in me because of who I was, not because I was me, it was still hard to adjust to the fact that now they didn't want to know me any more. I imagine it's the same for any athlete who's gone from being successful to being quite unsuccessful. When my career in football came to an end, I was 26 and I had a bit of an identity crisis. I'd been a footballer all my life, and now I wasn't and there was still a lot of life left to live. It was a pretty painful time, because when you want something ... then you get it quite early on, what is there left after that? I'd left school to play football – I didn't have much else.'

However, becoming a professional footballer wasn't the only crucial thing that happened to Richard the year he turned 16. That was also the year he became a Christian. 'I wasn't brought up in a Christian household, so I didn't really have any experience of it. I'd probably have described myself as Christian, but I had no idea what that actually meant. I thought Christianity was boring and Christians were weird; well, the ones I met seemed to be, and I was a footballer, so that wasn't for me. But then my sister became a Christian, and she wasn't weird. That really shook me. And I was intrigued.'

He went along to a few church services, and met his sister's Christian friends. 'They weren't weird, either. They had something that I didn't. I wanted to have what they had – although at the time I didn't know what it was. They kept talking about having a relationship with Jesus, and that he died on a cross for me. After a few months of investigating things for myself, I realised that I wasn't as great as I thought I was. I did need Jesus to die in my place, and so at 16 I decided to follow Jesus personally and became a Christian. At first I had no idea what I'd done. I thought being a Christian was just for Sundays, so I carried on my footballer's life quite happily: training, partying, and then making sure I was all right for 11 a.m. on Sunday morning. The longer I was a Christian, though, the more I realised that it affects your whole life. And gradually, the more I found out about the person of Jesus, the more I was wowed by him. I used to think Christianity was boring, but I came to see it as the most relevant, brilliant news – not just for me, but for everyone. My passion for football started to drain away, to be replaced by a passion for Jesus.'

Richard explains, 'I was probably about 19 or 20 when I really felt that I'd made the switch from wanting to be a professional footballer to wanting to be a professing Christian. Of course I was still a footballer, so I needed to keep that up, but football just didn't seem as important as it had been. I think in the end I just wasn't passionate enough about it any more, and as with any career, you've got to really want to do it. I didn't, and that's why I finished at 26. I guess my career was actually reflecting the changeover in my heart, as I went from being a footballer who went to church for an hour a week to a Christian who played football.'

Though Richard admits the move to being semi-professional and playing part-time rather than full-time was difficult, the change of lifestyle gave him the opportunity to take his new-found passion further, and study for a degree in theology at the University of Birmingham. He then worked for a church before further theological study led him to be ordained as a Church of England minister in 2010. He now works for a church in Birmingham, a job he is passionate about – the passion his football career was missing. He hasn't given up sport entirely, though. He plays five-a-side football, tennis, and is involved with Christians in Sport. 'I still love sport, and I do still play. I think I actually enjoy it more now than I did when I was professional. It sounds strange, but I always struggled with being paid to play. My wife is a passionate hockey player who pays to play. I used to say to her that when it's the other way round and you're paid to play, it goes from being a sport you love to a job. When it's a job, you're being paid to score goals, and if you don't score them, then you're sold to another club, or you're left out of the team. There were a lot of little things that together added up to the end of my career. But it all really stemmed from the fact that my heart wasn't really in it any more. Christianity had become more important to me than football.'

Richard's story isn't uncommon. For every athlete who breaks a world record, there are many more whose sporting careers simply come to a natural end. Richard, however, has no regrets. 'I'm very glad it turned out how it did. On one level it was the end of my career as a professional footballer, but on another God was working things out. I wouldn't change anything. There is nothing better than knowing the God who made you and serving him with your whole life ... not even a successful career in professional football can top that.'

CHAPTER 16

ERIC LIDDELL RUNNING

Crouching at the starting line, Eric composed himself. His running spikes dug into the ground. Flexing his muscles one last time, his head rose, waiting for the starting pistol. BANG! They were away first time. The 440 yard race was a strong event for Eric. Scotland was taking on their rivals England and Ireland at a meet in Stoke-on-Trent. It was the summer of 1923 and the sun was particularly warm that day. Beads of sweat formed on the athletes' foreheads even before the race began.

Eric was the favourite to win what was one of his strongest distances. He had started well, but the race was just about to get interesting. Literally jostling for first place, he was knocked out of his stride, tumbling, before hitting the ground with a heavy thud. The crowd gasped as they watched in horror. Their hero was surely out of the race. Time seemed to stand still as Eric hesitated. Looking up he saw the backs of his competitors; their heels flicking up behind them, sprinting towards the finish. But Eric was not finished yet. Rising to his feet he went after what seemed like an impossible target 20 yards ahead of him – the other athletes.

Regaining both his stride and his speed, Eric's own inimitable running style kicked in. His arms rotated like a helicopter rotor blade and his head dropped back like he was in the dentist's chair. With just yards to spare, Eric caught his opponents, and won the race.

He fell to the ground once again, this time with exhaustion. The crowd had just witnessed a truly great man, a gutsy athlete who wouldn't be brushed aside. Affectionately known as 'The Flying Scotsman', even today Eric Liddell is considered Scotland's greatest-ever athlete, being voted the most popular athlete Scotland has ever produced in *The Scotsman* newspaper in a 2008 poll.

Eric was one of four children born to Revd James Liddell and his wife. Working with the London Missionary Society, James and his family had given up their fairly affluent life and home in Edinburgh to move to Tianjin in northern China. It was in Tianjin that Eric and his older brother, Rob, were born. Eric was settled in China and studied at school there until his fifth birthday. His parents felt it would be best for his education if he and Rob returned to the UK for their schooling. Their younger sister, Jenny, and new baby brother, Ernest, would stay in China with his parents.

Rob and Eric enrolled at Eltham College, Mottingham, in south London. It was a boys' boarding school for children whose parents were Christian missionaries around the world. Being around people who were in the same family situation was good for Eric, and he loved the competitiveness of a boys' school, especially when it came to sport, in which he, naturally, excelled.

His mum and dad, along with Jenny and little Ernest, would return home every few years for an extended holiday. They would go back to Edinburgh, catching up with family and friends.

At Eltham, Eric Liddell was an outstanding sportsman. No matter what he turned his hand to on the sports fields, he always excelled. A fine cricketer, Eric soon became captain of the school's first XI, as well as captain of the first XV. When it came to games, Eric was always the person people wanted in their team. He was the first person to be chosen, every time. He was simply a brilliant sportsman. If anyone at school was unsure of his ability, it was confirmed by the school when they awarded him the Blackheath Cup – given to the best athlete of the year.

News of this extraordinary young athlete soon travelled far and wide, and the newspaper journalists' excitement was tangible as they wrote column inch after column inch about this new-found star, covering his achievements at various sporting events around the country. He was well known for being the fastest runner in Scotland, and many wondered if he would be a potential Olympic winner, the first in Scottish history.

And yet there was something different about this wiry Scotsman. Unassuming and self-effacing, Liddell was a likeable character. None of his talent, or indeed his success, had gone to his head. He loved what he did, and what he achieved, but he acknowledged his gift was God-given.

There was indeed something different about this man. The glory was not to be for him, but for his God. His headmaster described him as being 'entirely without vanity'.

It was his firm and vocal faith that led Eric to be asked to speak at various places about Christianity. He was an earnest speaker, and it was hoped that his high profile would help bring people to the meetings.

In the autumn of 1920, Eric followed his brother Rob to the University of Edinburgh to study pure science. It was here that his athletics and rugby career really began to soar. He could devote more time to it, and the opportunities were endless. Though the facilities at Eltham were good, they didn't compare to those at university. Despite the athletics track and rugby pitches now available to him, Eric could often be seen in the distance, on the peaks of the hills, running wild and free.

It was no surprise to anybody when Eric was selected to run for the university, representing it in the 100 and 220 yard races, winning most of the events he attended (while also fitting in playing Rugby Union for the national side, in the Five Nations).

Athletics was his first love, however, and so not surprisingly received most of his attention. He was now running the 100 yards so fast that in 1924 he set a new British record of 9.7 seconds: a record that would not be broken for the next thirty-five years.

Keen to honour all areas of his university life, Eric graduated with a Bachelor of Science degree in 1924.

In that same year as his graduation, there was to be an event that would make Eric Liddell a household name far beyond his own generation: the famous Paris Olympiad. Eric was selected to represent his country as always, and was a key figure in the British team. To have an athlete of his magnitude is always good for the squad. He commanded, though not demanded, respect, and he received it from all quarters.

The schedule for the games had been released some months before, and there was a problem. The heats of Eric's best event, the 100 metres, were to be held on a Sunday. As a committed Christian, Eric refused to run. An athlete refusing to run was unheard of. This was the Olympics. People don't refuse to run in the Olympics. However, Liddell's beliefs and morals went far beyond a gold medal. Not even when under pressure from the British governing body for athletics would Eric change his mind.

Years earlier, while still a child in China, Eric had become a Christian. He was taught by his parents about the Bible and the Christian life, and though very young, committed his life to Jesus. Though it perhaps didn't become a tangible, visible belief until he was at Eltham, and increasingly so at university in Edinburgh, there was no doubting it now – Eric was committed to living life under the rule of Jesus. Growing up in a Christian family no doubt helped Eric. Nevertheless, this was not an inherited faith. It was real, and his decision to put God above gold was proof. For Eric, putting Jesus first by not running on a Sunday was the natural response to what Jesus had done for him. Though Eric was a superstar of that day, a natural-born winner, he was still a sinner. He still did wrong things. And he knew that he fell short of God's expectations. He needed Jesus' forgiveness, which he offers through his death on the cross. It was the understanding and acceptance of this as a young boy in China that was now impacting the life of this world-renowned athlete, now in his twenties.

Knowing the schedule ahead of time, Liddell spent the intervening months training hard for the 400 metres, which was not on Sunday, and was an event in which he had previously excelled. Even so, no one expected him to have much success. The British governing body was not overly impressed at his decision not to run in the 100 metres, but they would rather see him run in the 400 metres than not at all.

Eric made it through his heats and found himself in the final. Before the event, the British team's masseur handed him a note of support which quoted 'He that honours me, I will honour', referring to the passage in the Bible at 1 Samuel 2:30.

Not only did he win the race, but he smashed the world record and replaced it with a time of 47.6 seconds. God had indeed honoured Liddell's commitment not to run on Sunday.

A few days earlier Liddell had competed in the 200 metre finals, finishing third behind Americans Jackson

Scholz and Charles Paddock, beating old rival Harold Abrahams, who finished in sixth place. This would be the second and final time these two competitors would meet.

Though a national hero and sporting champion, Eric was keen to return to his 'homeland' of China, and the people whom he loved. Within a year of winning gold, he was boarding a boat to China. He would spend time first in the province of Tianjin where he was born, teaching at an Anglo-Chinese college, before moving to Shaochang. While he was still competing sporadically (but still at the top level), his work was now very different.

Life was hard for the now married Eric, a far cry from the comfort of Edinburgh. In 1941, China was such a dangerous place to live that the British government were advising British nationals to leave, unless their presence was absolutely essential. Eric was now helping his brother Rob, who was a doctor. The conditions were poor and Rob was desperately in need of a break. Eric felt unable and unwilling to leave his brother, despite the risk to his own life. Instead he said goodbye to his wife and three girls, who returned to his wife's homeland of Canada, and he stayed at the mission station in Shaochang.

Eric's presence meant a little respite for his brother. He was a great help to Rob – even once running so fast he was able to catch a wild hare, a blessing considering they were living on war rations.

Eric's final years of life were spent far from home, from comfort, and a long way from family. In a letter to his wife, written on the day he died, he spoke about finding life increasingly difficult, and suffering what he thought was a nervous breakdown due to overwork. In fact, he was suffering from an inoperable brain tumour; being overworked and malnourished probably hastened his demise. He died later that same day, 21 February 1945. All of Scotland mourned.

Eric will be remembered for a number of things: his speed, his records, his medals, but most of all his determination to honour God by refusing to run on Sundays. For some it was fanatical, for others it left them bewildered. However, for Eric Liddell it was an act of obedience to God and a sign of his faith to millions around the world. The man who gave up the chance to race gained more than any competition could bring. He later gave his life to reach those whom he loved – the people of China.

EPILOGUE

Even if you have read just a couple of stories from this book, you'll know that while a love for sport and a desire to win feature high in the sportspeople's priorities, there is something much bigger and deeper that motivates and moves them.

Whether they are a household name, or just played for their local side, each of them has something in common: they have all, at some point in their life, become a Christian.

For some readers, that might sound a bit odd. Others might take the approach that 'It's OK for them, but not for me,' while some might see the change that trusting in Jesus has made in the lives of the people they have read about, and want to know more.

I have seven nephews and I remember each one of them being born. Not that I was there at the actual moment, but I recall them being brought home for the first time. Their parents were proud, and rightly so. The day the babies arrived in this world, everything changed for their family. For their parents came huge responsibility, great love and fondness, disturbed sleep, not to mention the smell that wafted through the house because of dirty nappies. With one little baby's arrival their whole world was turned upside down, never to be the same again.

In a similar way, as we have seen in these true stories, life can never be the same for a person when they really understand who Jesus is and why he came. When he comes into a life, things change for the better. This has always been the way. When Jesus walked the earth around 2,000 years ago he met countless people, and when they really encountered who he was and what he wanted to do for them, their lives were turned upside down. For example, there were the thousands of hungry people on a mountainside with no food – and yet from one small lunch Jesus fed them all. Sounds a bit mysterious, but read about it for yourself in Mark's Gospel, chapter 6, verses 31–44. Those hungry people were never the same again after that experience.

Or take the man who was paralyzed. His friends carried him on his bed to meet Jesus. And when he got there, Jesus forgave his sins and cured his illness. When he encountered Jesus, his life was changed. Check out Matthew 9:1–8 for the full story.

What about the little girl who had died? All her family were crying and mourning, clustered around her body. Jesus walked into the room, told the girl to get up, and without so much as receiving mouth-to-mouth resuscitation, she did so, and went on with life. Amazing as it might sound, the little girl's life and all her family's were changed when they met Jesus (see Luke 8:40–42,49–56).

Let's have a look at one more example. Because when we look at this person, we'll find out a lot about Jesus, but also a lot about ourselves too.

We pick up the story as Jesus is travelling by a lake.

A large crowd came to him, and he began to teach them. As he walked along, he saw Levi son of Alphaeus sitting at the tax collector's booth. 'Follow me,' Jesus told him, and Levi got up and followed him. While Jesus was having dinner at Levi's house, many tax collectors and 'sinners' were eating with him and his disciples, for there were many who followed him. When the teachers of the law who were Pharisees saw him eating with the 'sinners' and tax collectors, they asked his disciples: 'Why does he eat with tax collectors and "sinners"?' On hearing this, Jesus said to them, 'It is not the healthy who need a doctor, but the sick. I have not come to call the righteous, but sinners.' (Mk. 2:13–17)

Back then, tax collectors were despised. They were crooks, dishonest in their dealings and happy to steal for their own gain. Levi, or Matthew, was just like any other tax collector in biblical times. He stole from people, and looked after himself at others' expense. It was clear to all that he was what the Bible calls 'a sinner'. Levi had done wrong in his life – and a lot of it. And yet as Jesus walked by the lake, with a large crowd following him, he stopped and made a special point of calling him.

All we have in the story above is that Jesus stopped by Levi's table and told him to follow him, and yet Levi got up, left everything and followed Jesus. No doubt Levi had heard of all that Jesus had been doing and teaching: healing the sick, feeding the hungry, and changing people's lives. Though he had plenty of money, Levi knew this wasn't everything. Though he had a career, he knew this didn't satisfy, and so like the people in this book, Levi responded to Jesus' call and followed him.

This was not a small, insignificant step for Levi. It was not a religious fashion accessory – this was a call on his life that would change everything.

It affected his job: did you spot that Levi got up from his tax-collecting booth? Following Jesus meant a career change. No longer was he to be a crook, fiddling other people's tax bills for his own gain. Now Jesus was to be boss in his life, and Levi was to have a new job. It affected his friends: as Jesus became Lord of Levi's life it meant that he now had new friends. In getting up from his desk, Levi was turning his back on living for himself and his own priorities. As soon as Jesus walked into Levi's life, his social calendar changed. While previously he was selfish, a thief, now he opened up his home and held a dinner for people like himself – who, as the Bible describes, were once lost, but had been found and brought 'home' after an encounter with Jesus (see the story of the Lost Son in Luke 15:11–32).

When a person accepts what Jesus has done for them, it might mean a change of career, and will no doubt affect their friends – but ultimately and most importantly, when Jesus takes charge he changes every area of their life. Jesus is not some religious dictator, or unkind ruler who just puts restrictions on people. When Jesus comes into a person's heart by his Holy Spirit he sets us free, gives us peace and brings a new purpose to life. The Bible tells us, 'if the Son [Jesus] sets you free, you will be free indeed' (Jn. 8:36). This is a promise from Jesus himself.

Jesus came to earth not just to perform amazing miracles or to teach inspirational things. He came to save and rescue people who without him are lost, with no hope for eternity in heaven. Jesus came ultimately to die a death he didn't deserve to bring us forgiveness for the wrong things we have done. You and I may not be deliberately ripping people off and stealing from them the way Levi was, but if we are honest, we know we aren't the people we should be. We aren't the people God wants us to be and we need his forgiveness.

The Bible says that when we look for God, we will find him if we look with all our heart. He is a God who wants to be found. He's a God who wants to change lives and he does this by forgiving us, changing us, and becoming the good and loving boss of our lives (see Jer. 29:11–13). He has great plans for us, whether we are successful sportspeople or are happy enough just watching from the sidelines. With Jesus, everyone is a winner.

If the stories have challenged you, and you would like to ask Jesus to come into your life, why not pray the prayer that I did:

Dear God, I have really messed up. My life feels ruined in so many ways, and I have so many regrets. Please will you forgive me? I have been running from you for ages. I can't change myself. I am trusting in you, trusting you can and will. Thank you.

If you have been able to say this prayer, then share what you have done with someone else – perhaps a trusted Christian friend or minister, or the person who gave you this book. Alternatively, contact me, Jonathan Carswell, c/o info@10ofthose.com.

10Publishing is the publishing house of **10ofThose**.
It is committed to producing quality Christian
resources that are biblical and accessible.

www.10ofthose.com is our online retail arm selling
thousands of quality books at discounted prices.

For information contact: **info@10ofthose.com**
or check out our website: **www.10ofthose.com**